GUIDELINES FOR
CONTEMPORARY CATHOLICS:
Sexuality

GUIDELINES FOR CONTEMPORARY CATHOLICS:
Sexuality

Mary G. Durkin

THE THOMAS MORE PRESS
Chicago, Illinois

ISBN 0-88347-211-2

CONTENTS

INTRODUCTION

God created man in the image of himself, in the image of God he created him, male and female he created them.

Genesis 1:27

God saw all he had made, and indeed it was very good.

Genesis 1:31

It's a basic fact of human existence that at every time and in every place, God created humans male and female.

Pope John Paul II

The real force of the teaching of the Church's tradition, culminating in *Humanae Vitae* and so often reasserted by Pope John Paul II, lies in seeing that the connection between intercourse and procreation is the very linchpin of societal sexual morality, and once this connection is broken, there is no real basis for any kind of restraint. If contraceptive relations are morally acceptable in marriage, why not outside of marriage?

Archbishop Pilarczyk

A STORY illustrates the problems encountered in a discussion of religious guidelines for sexuality:

A women's magazine requested an article on "Religion

7

and Sexuality.'' My co-author and I wrote about the mystery we humans encounter in our experiences of sexuality, about how religion has offered interpretations of that mystery in light of the understandings and needs of specific periods in human history, about how oftentimes these understandings were based on a cultural bias against women, about how even in a time of increased scientific understanding there is still confusion about the meaning of sexuality, and finally about how religion might offer some inspiration that would dispel this confusion.

The editor rejected the article as we had written it. She wanted it reworked to demonstrate how religion was THE cause of all the problems people are experiencing with their sexuality. We made some changes in our original article; but when we refused to make religion the scapegoat for our society's confusion about sexuality, she turned down our work.

After all, she *knew* that religion was the cause of our confusion about sex. All her friends—and especially her Catholic friends—had horror stories about what priests and nuns and other religious leaders had told them about sex. If only they could rid themselves of the guilt these educators had instilled in them, they would be able to lead sexually fulfilling lives.

The only logical response to her and to the legions like her who want to trace all their sexually related difficulties to the doorstep of religion is: ''You're wrong.''

Of course, organized religion can be faulted for many of its attitudes regarding sex; but to blame religion for all the contemporary confusion about sexuality is a sign of either naivete or scientific and historical ignorance. Human sexuality—the fact that humans come with bodies that are attracted to and attracted by other bodies in a way that offers the possibility of emotional commitment—is a basic, complex, and pervasive characteristic of the human way of being in this world. Something this basic, this complex, this pervasive characteristic confronts humans with mystery, with the possibility of choice (either for good or for bad), with a never-ending quest for understanding.

The desire to blame one social institution for all sex-related problems has a corollary in the desire to find *the* once and for all, final, complete answer about how to be a sexual being which keeps the modern publishing and advertising businesses flourishing. Neither desire is rooted in a true appraisal of the situation.

Guidelines for sexuality that are rooted in a Catholic understanding will be helpful only if they are a response to a realistic understanding of sexuality. Before attempting to discuss sexuality guidelines for contemporary Catholics it is necessary to consider the basic nature of sexuality and why it always has been closely linked with religion. In other words, the starting point must be an examination of the experience of sexuality, considering both scientific and historical investigations of its role in human experience.

Although both religion and the contemporary world seem to concentrate on sex when sexuality is discussed, it is essential for the development of guidelines to appreciate that sexuality is more than sex. Both church leaders and self-proclaimed sex experts seem to concentrate their attention on erotic behavior and, to a lesser degree, reproduction, ignoring the fact that sexuality influences other aspects of human life. An integrated sexual identity, which would contribute to a sexually fulfilling life, requires the inclusion of more than the narrow focus of much of the past and present discussions about sexuality.

For the purposes of this study, once we have identified

what we mean by sexuality, we will review the history of the church's response to the mystery of sexuality. We will survey both the scriptures and the tradition of the church, examining both the major strain that has often been negative in its evaluation of sexuality and the minor strain that recognizes the sacramentality of sexuality. We will then consider the present-day position of the magisterium on sexuality-related issues as well as contemporary secular and theological discussions of sexuality. The response of the laity and lower clergy to both the magisterium and to their own experiences of themselves as sexual beings will also be investigated before we conclude with some suggestions for how the richness of the Catholic sacramental perspective might be a positive force for helping us live as sexually mature human beings.

We will not concentrate on the church's teachings on specific moral activities. Our thesis is that guidelines for contemporary Catholics need to move beyond a legal approach to sexuality in order to discover its true meaning. Once a meaning of sexuality surfaces, the values apparent in that meaning can be used to evaluate behavior. Our approach will demonstrate how the church's emphasis on the law and its anti-woman, anti-sex mentality have been a deterrent to the development of a positive Catholic imagination on sexuality. What is sorely lacking in both the church's and the secular world's approaches to sexuality is a vision that challenges people to an integrated sexual identity grounded in an appreciation of the enormous influence sexuality has on human life. Our study of sexuality will show the direction in which Catholicism must move if it wants to develop such a vision.

A process of co-relation is the method used here in de-

veloping sexuality guidelines for Catholics. This theological method seeks to bring together human experience
and faith in a way that leads to a deeper understanding of
both experience and faith. God is seen as present in both
the ordinary and extra-ordinary experiences of human life,
oftentimes waiting to be recognized as the manifestation of
what is professed in the creed. When this recognition occurs, both the experience and the creed take on increased
significance. The role of the theologian and pastoral leader
is to call attention to the activity of God in human experience, encouraging others to recognize the grace-filled
possibilities of the experience.

This method of co-relation rejects a rules and regulations approach that is not related to the actual experience
to which it speaks. The archbishop quoted at the beginning
of this chapter demonstrates what happens when representatives of the magisterium fail to understand the situation
they seek to address. The quote is taken from an attempt to
present the church's teaching in a way that is "understand-
able and persuasive to Christian believers of our time."

The response of most married people to the quote would
probably be similar to that of a woman I know who angrily
asked, "Does he think that the only thing that would keep
us faithful is the possibility of pregnancy? Why don't they
ever ask us about what goes on in our marriages before
they make such stupid statements?"

Instead of handing down rules from on high, the method
of co-relation suggests that when people recognize the God
that is present in their lives through a co-relation of life
and faith, they can be moved to evaluate their experiences
in light of this God. The pastoral leader—be it the pope, a
bishop, or a local church worker—needs to facilitate the

process whereby church members can be reminded that their experience of God's presence points them towards behavior that will increase the divine presence in their own lives and help them to be witnesses for others of the possibility of this presence. Guidelines for sexuality are meant to encourage individual and communal consideration of what God's presence in the experience of sexuality has to say about behavior that might testify to this presence.

Those in secular culture who want to blame religion for all human sexual problems and those in the church who concentrate on erotic behavior and reproduction when they speak about sexuality will probably reject this "guidelines" approach. More than likely both the editor of the women's magazine and the archbishop would be opposed to co-relation. The editor and those who share her perspective claim that religion should stay out of the bedroom: it has no business there and only causes problems because it tries to coerce people into correct sexual behavior. The archbishop's view encourages the position of many religious people that the church should be the policeman in the bedroom because humankind is unable to control its sexual behavior. The co-relationist believes that the mystery of human sexuality with both its positive and demonic possibilities requires an "explanation" that can be found in the richness of a religious perspective. Guidelines that develop out of this explanation should aim to help individuals appreciate the meaning of human sexuality discovered in the co-relation of faith and experience. In this view, religion belongs in the bedroom as inspiration and challenge.

Catholic discussion of sexuality must strive to discover how to best articulate this inspiration and challenge.

PART ONE

CHAPTER I
The Situation: An Overview

We were conceived in the animal world but came to maturity under the influence of a self-generating culture.

Richard Leakey

Sexuality is more than sex.

AMA Statement on Sexuality

FROM time to time some social commentator will wonder: "Why is the Catholic Church so obsessed with sex?" At the same time, religious leaders decry the secular culture's obsession with sex. And, periodically, individuals find themselves wondering about their own or other people's obsession with sex. Why is it, they wonder, that sex is such an obsession that it seems to be the main focus of statements by a major religious body and by the biggest sellers of everything from cars to clothing, as well as the surprise that often interferes with our best laid plans? Animals don't seem to have any problems with their sex drive, and yet those who supposedly are the "higher" animal seem dominated by sex.

Traditionally, religion has offered an explanation for the mystery experienced in our sexuality; it has deprived the mystery of its terror and helped humans make some sense out of their powerful sexual drive. Unfortunately, Religion (organized religion with a capital "R") and religion (one's

15

ultimate meaning system) also have often robbed sexuality of the wonder that is contained in its mystery and reduced the sexual drive to little more than an instinct.

The challenge for those hoping to develop a religious perspective that offers guidelines for sexuality in today's world is to recognize that sexuality is a pervasive power in many facets of human life. Without an understanding of the human need for an integrated sexual identity, there will never be a true appreciation of the meaning of human sexuality. Once there is a recognition that sexuality is an intellectual, physical, cultural, and personal phenomenon, the complexity of human sexuality becomes apparent. Sex is an obsession because of its unacknowledged complexity and because its mystery is no longer so surprising.

Human Sexuality/Animal Sexuality

Human sexuality is similar to, but also different from, animal sexuality. Though there are physical differences between the two, the crucial difference lies in the human's unique intellectual capacities. Before examining the physical basis of the differences between human and animal sexuality, it is necessary to consider two features of humankind's intellectual make-up that make our sexuality unique: 1) we are able to make choices, and 2) we are meaning-creating animals.

Unlike the other primates, humans are able to choose how to use their sexuality. This ability to choose is at times experienced as a blessing and at other times as a curse. When the way we respond to our sexual potential leads to positive results, we rejoice. When we are devastated by misuse of our sexuality, we wish that we had been created differently.

When the powerful sexual drive propels two people towards union and helps them form a bond that allows them to grow in their capacity for intimacy—both physical and psychological intimacy—we marvel. We see how sexuality helps humans overcome the self-centeredness that is the result of an equally strong human desire, the desire for independence.

We see this marvel at a wedding where two people, caught up in the throes of romantic love (I call it erotic-romantic love, because it grows out of sexual desire), eagerly commit themselves to each other, disregarding all the obvious obstacles that could interfere with their dream of a lifetime together. We shake our heads, think that love is blind, and secretly envy their enthusiasm for each other and for life.

But when the sexual drive leads to obvious manipulation of others, seeing them only as objects for one's satisfaction, we recoil. This other side of the coin of our sexuality seems a mockery of the human capacity for romance. We also are reminded of how often we use our sexuality in a manipulative way.

Kiddie porn, wife abuse, sexual discrimination, and prostitution are examples of societal behavior that uses sex as a means of manipulation. While we might not support these practices, we know that there are times when we use our sexuality with little regard for the personhood of the other—perhaps seeing another as a stereotype rather than acknowledging his/her personal worth—and we are disturbed by our behavior.

We are also meaning-creating animals. Our genetic programming inclines us towards behavior, but in most instances—including sexually related activities—we must impose meaning on what we do or face confusion and disorder. In other words, we continually ask "why" certain things are the way they are and why we behave in the way we do. When we don't find the answer to our why, or when we try to live without even asking the why, the result is both personal and societal disintegration.

For too long both religion and society ignored the positive force of sexuality when seeking to answer the "why." The meaning of sexuality proposed by these institutions failed to acknowledge that sexuality has an enriching power that allows people to develop their capacity for intimacy. Instead, the explanations for human sexuality centered on its similarity to animal sexuality. The reproductive function of sexuality was the primary focus; any pleasure associated with the sexual act was allowed only if it did not interfere with the survival of the family, clan, community or state.

At the same time, humans who have sought pleasure in their sexual activities have been branded as "animals," a designation that was quite unfair to animals. Actually, if reproduction is the only purpose for sexuality, animals are quite responsible sexual beings. They are interested in mating only when reproduction is possible. They are genetically programmed to behave in this manner, and they have no difficulty responding to this programming.

An examination of modern scientific discoveries about the evolution of human sexuality coupled with an investigation of how various "self-generating cultures" have responded to the possibilities of human sexuality reveals that for us, sexuality is more than sex—more than a biological instinct to mate—and more than a means of reproduction for our species.

Conceived in an Animal World

Though we were conceived in the animal world, human sexuality is still genetically unique. While the other primates limit their mating to those times with reproductive possibilities, humans are interested in and capable of mating even when reproduction is not a possibility. According to primatologists, sociobiologists, and physical anthropologists, this distinctively human characteristic led to the survival of our species when the movement into new environments required an extended period for teaching survival techniques to the next generation. The young required a "secure" environment in which to acquire an expertise that was not instinctive.

The secondary sex characteristics of the female—her sexiness—along with her willingness to mate at any time allowed the formation of an emotional bond between the mother and the father of a child, at least for the period of childbearing and childrearing, thus offering their offspring a greater chance of survival. The pleasure of sexual union, along with the ability to remember this pleasure and to fantasize about this pleasure, resulted in a quasi pairbonding propensity in human sexuality. In other words, the drive toward pleasurable physical union is part of our genetic makeup; but we are not determined in how we act in response to this drive. We are free to form a bond or to ignore the bonding possibilities in a sexual union.

Some anthropologists believe that the bonding potential

between the human male and female formed very early on in hominid history. In our species the bond was strong enough to support the survival of *homo sapiens* when the movement out of the forest and into the plains required more than instinctive abilities.

While early human sexuality did not result in monogamy, it appears that human males only mated with the number of females they were able to protect during pregnancy and childrearing. Emotional bonds did form between the partners in these relationships. Even if these early bonds were not like those of contemporary romantic lovers, the potential for the latter was present in the former, genetically influenced, response to sexual attraction.

So it can be said of humans that we have a genetic propensity to form a bond with those with whom we mate, a propensity that has its origins in our early hominid ancestors, a propensity that is very powerful, but that is also open to choice. And we make our choices based on our understanding of the meaning of sexuality. For, as Leakey indicates in our opening quotation, we came to maturity in self-generating cultures that assigned meaning to the sexual attraction and to our bonding possibilities. While these self-generating cultures might have come to different understandings of the meaning of human sexuality, one thing remains constant in every human culture: sexuality has had a profound influence on human behavior, an influence that has gone beyond its reproductive power. Human sexuality is more than sex.

The "more" of human sexuality offers us our greatest challenge. Human sexuality is filled with possibilities for the individual, the family, the community, the survival of humankind; but at the same time our freedom to choose how to use our sexuality—an important dimension of the same "more"—can cause devastation for us, our families, our communities and for the possibilities of emotional growth in our cultures. Much of both our understanding of human sexuality and our evaluation of sexually-related behavior is rooted in an appreciation of human sexuality that predominated in previous eras of human history. Knowing how and why those who preceded us responded to the "more" of human sexuality sheds some light on the problems we have when we try to uncover a meaning to our sexuality in this contemporary world.

Self-Generating Cultures

Throughout human history our self-generating cultures have emphasized the reproductive dimension of sexuality, subordinating all other possibilities to the need for community survival. Sexual pleasure was allowed only when the survival of the society was not threatened by erotic practices both inside and outside of marriage (or an equivalent arrangement that assured the conception and rearing of children). However, sexual pleasure was not seen as helpful to the bonding of sexual partners, but rather it was viewed as something apart from sexual union with the other parent of an offspring.

We find examples of sexual pleasure divorced from intimacy and sex in marriage divorced from sexual pleasure in societies as divergent as pre-Christian Rome and fifteenth century France. In the literature of ancient Rome the love of boys (by men) was evaluated as the same as the love of women. Some men chose women, others chose boys, and still others chose both for their sexual pleasure. The right-ness of this search for pleasure was evaluated by a thinker based on his view of the legitimacy of love and passion. Some felt that all forms of passion were uncontrollable and destructive of a man's physical and mental powers. For example, homosexuality was condemned only if a citizen (a male) assumed a passive—that is a feminine—role in the relationship.

In the latter part of the fifteenth century, public prostitution in French towns attested to the movement from prostitution being merely tolerated to prostitution being what one commentator calls "encouraged municipalized fornication." The municipal brothel was looked upon as a "tranquilizing agency," supposedly an alternative to sexual assaults on women, who were often wrongly accused of behavior that would make them easy targets for roving gangs of males intent on sexual satisfaction. However, these brothels served many of the town's leading citizens, including its clergy. And this in a society that paid tribute to the family ideal!

Marriage and the faithfulness of a wife assured a man that he was not cuckold. The continuation of the male line was guaranteed when bonding was seen as the requirement that a woman be faithful to her husband. Sexual pleasure and emotional bonding were not necessarily part of the marriage contract designed to assure reproduction. Pleasure could be sought in other places—in Rome in relationships with other males and in French towns with a prostitute. Obviously women were not held in high regard in these societies, nor were they accorded this respect in the other patriarchal societies that have exercised such a great influence on our contemporary understanding of sexuality.

Because it was subject to societal mores geared to assure reproduction, the bonding potential of human sexuality never acquired an equal footing with either sexual pleasure or reproduction. In other words, when the meaning of sexuality was determined by the economic requirement of population growth, the uniquely human dimension of sexuality was ignored.

In this atmosphere it was necessary to "control" the powerful sexual drive so it would serve societal needs. The search for sexual pleasure gone awry would be devastating for the future of the society. Explanations of sexuality sought to assure that enough children would survive to replace the adults of the community. Since for most of human history it was necessary for a woman to have ten pregnancies and at least seven live births in order for even two offspring to survive to replace her and her mate, the continuation of any community—the family, the kinship group, the clan, the state—required rigid control of sexual behavior. Even those societies that seem to have lax attitudes towards sexual pleasure (for the males) outside of marriage, did so only after reproductive survival was assured. Societies depended on the willingness of women to spend most of their adult lives in pregnancy and the willingness of the men to care for the women and their offspring.

Rules governed behavior to assure that a man was not cuckold and that offspring were cared for. The importance placed on the male's offspring demanded faithfulness from the wife, but did not deter a husband from seeking sexual pleasure outside of marriage. The male orientation of a society's rules in this regard are exemplified in the rulers' response to the church's attempt to require fidelity on the part of the husbands of the ruling class as well as on the part of their wives. The secular rulers supported the church in its restraint on women but refused to accept the church's prohibition for men. Again, emotional bonding between parents was not considered essential; only reproduction was important.

This is not to claim that emotional bonding did not occur between spouses in previous cultures. There is ample evidence in literature of the discovery of the bonding potential of sexuality even when the societal mores did not encourage this bonding. Still, for most of human history, reproduction was a paramount concern and the primary meaning of sexuality was determined by this concern. When the meaning of sexuality centered on its reproductive potential, the uniqueness of human sexuality was never allowed to flourish. Instead a stilted and fragmented understanding of sexuality was the norm.

In a society that emphasized reproduction, the role of men and the role of women were closely linked to their reproductive tasks. In the patriarchal societies which predominated once the fruits of the male's hunting and fishing became the medium of exchange, men assumed control of the society and were accorded a "higher" place than women. They were the active force in the society. Even though women bore the next generation (some modern commentators would say because women performed an essential task that men could not), their work was considered inferior. Women were looked upon as passive and subordinate, incapable of rational thought.

The roles of men and women were reinforced by both religious and secular myths that emphasized stereotypes of male and female sexuality viewed as reproductive capability. Myths supply the rationale for certain behavior, especially when the behavior is related to that which is mysterious or not easily understood.

At the same time, unexamined myths often persist long after they have any relationship to reality, because they exercise a powerful hold on our imaginations, especially when the myths remove any threat we might feel when we face the mysterious. This is especially true about myths that "explain" human sexuality since even our advanced scientific knowledge has not eradicated the mystery from human sexuality. As the theologian David Tracy observed, "Sexuality is probably the last great outpost of the extraordinary in human experience."

The primary myth of male/female roles is summarized in the often repeated dictum: "Man's work is in the world; Woman's place is in the home." This belief, which dictated male and female behavior in most patriarchal cultures, shows the pervasive influence of sexuality in human society. In addition, the myth's effects demonstrate how an overemphasis on reproduction as the primary meaning of sexuality interfered with both women's and men's potential to behave differently than the stereotype's expectations. The attitude encouraged by this myth shows the importance of the pronouncement by the American Medical Association that sexuality is more than sex, more than erotic behavior and reproduction.

The Contemporary Situation:
More than Sex

An overview of the situation of human sexuality must include an examination of how its uniqueness permeates all aspects of our lives, both personal and social. The American Medical Association pronouncement emphasizes that human sexuality is more than what we do. It is also "an identification, an activity, a drive, a biological and emotional process, an outlook and an expression of the self." As such, human sexuality is "an important factor in every personal relationship, in every human endeavor, from business to politics."

Building on this statement, the Committee for Human Sexual Development has identified seven areas of human experience that are influenced by the fact that we humans come with bodies that have a powerful attraction to other bodies. These seven areas are: 1) our bodily self image; 2) the ways in which we give and receive affection; 3) our conception of male and female roles; 4) our expectations for family lifestyles; 5) the way in which we act as sex educators; 6) our erotic activities; and 7) our reproductive behavior.

Sexual maturity requires that behavior in one of these areas be consistent with behavior in all other areas, a difficult task at best. For example, if we believe in equality of the sexes, then we should not engage in erotic activities that treat a person of the other sex as a mere object for our enjoyment. Or if we have a negative bodily self-image, we probably will find it difficult to be a good sex educator, no matter how sexually free we might think we are. Guidelines for sexuality ought to assist a person as s/he attempts to develop an integrated sexual identity.

The pervasiveness of human sexuality, its profound influence on the way we live, on the way we relate to others, on our sense of who we are, is obvious when we reflect on our experiences with an understanding of sexuality as more than sex. Given the complexity of human sexuality, it is little wonder that individuals and societies—both in the past and in the present—have been confounded by its challenge. Using the Committee on Human Sexual Development categories, we begin to grasp the influence of sexuality on human behavior.

Bodily Self-Image

A visitor from Ireland expressed her amazement at the number of obese people she observed on the streets of Chicago, a fact more obvious since she was here during a warm spell in late spring. She remarked on the contrast between the image she had formed from watching television commercials—Americans are obsessed with being fit, she thought—and the reality she witnessed.

Obviously not all Chicagoans are obese, nor are all Americans overweight. Still, our Irish visitor's comment on the difference between the media image of the perfect body and the reality points up the difficulties many of us have with our bodily self-image. While we might all long to be "tens," we know that few people have been blessed with the genes that will allow us to do more than wish for that perfection.

Our image of our attractiveness is influenced by the media presentation of an alluring person of the same sex. If we are women, we wish for a perfect figure, for gleaming hair, for a well proportioned face, for a sexy walk, for captivating eyes. If we are men, we wish we could convey the macho image of the Marlboro Man. In short, our bodily self-image is conditioned by our sexual identity. We long to be sexy, and it is this longing that the advertising world capitalizes on so successfully.

Yet even when we have passed the adolescent stage of total despair over our bodies, few of us are completely at ease with our bodies. The adolescent despair is obviously linked to the body's sexual development. So, too, the adult's discomfort with his/her body often springs from an inability to accept the body's sexuality as something good. The Manichean distaste for the body survives in all of us, and our less than "perfect" bodies—at least when compared with the media idols—tend to reinforce that distaste.

Also our bodies are apt to betray us with their sexual longings. When we are least prepared to feel a sexual attraction, we are surprised by our reactions to another person. Or when a partner wants us to be responsive, something interferes with our ability to react. Since our bodies are not to be trusted, we often develop a bodily self-hatred that manifests itself in the way we ignore our potential bodily charm.

The American desire for bodily well-being is the positive side of our collective view of the body. The dark side of this view is the distaste we often feel toward our own bodies.

Giving and Receiving Affection

If we are uncertain about our bodies and question their tendency to betray us, we can find the giving and receiving of affection—especially when these include bodily contact

—threatening. Silent messages about appropriate ways of expressing affection are given from the time we are very young. The family, the school, and the media contribute to our ideas about what is acceptable and what is unacceptable, often linking this to sexual identity.

For example, in most media presentations women are allowed to be tender with other women and with men, while men are expected to be macho with both other men and with women. In a family this attitude is reinforced with the message, "Big boys don't cry." Also when boys reach a certain age, it no longer is appropriate for them to kiss their fathers. And physical contact between men, except in sporting activities, is frowned upon in most sectors of our society as is a public excessive show of affection between a man and a woman who are not married, especially if they are married to other people.

The linking of affection with the possible arousal of sexual desire has put constraints on both individuals and society. Given the human need for affection, these constraints can have a devastating effect. One woman's experience demonstrates how fear of sexual desire influences how we give and receive affection. She says she has no memory of ever being hugged or kissed by her mother, a hard-working and cold Irish farm woman. When she was very small, her father would periodically hold her on his knee; but once she became a pre-adolescent, this only sign of familial affection ceased. Now she realizes that a fear of sexual desire controlled the giving and receiving of affection in her family. It is little wonder that this woman has had a difficult time forming emotional bonds in her adult life.

Male/Female Roles

The myth of man's world and woman's place is no longer a correct interpretation of the situation in our technological world. Still, the stereotypes that this myth engendered have a strong influence on our imaginations. Women might be able to do most of the tasks of our work world and men might be involved in parenting, but sexual differentiation persists as a force in our sense of who we are. Even the most non-sexist men and women have subconscious and often unacknowledged expectations about what is appropriate male and female behavior.

Although anatomy is no longer destiny, the idea of the superiority of male activities and of the male's greater intellectual ability and physical powers supports those who wish to keep women in a subservient position. Presidential advisors speak of women's lack of interest in political issues, church leaders cite theology as the basis for the non-ordination of women, high school boys abuse a young woman who qualifies to play football, and women are routinely subjected to sexual abuse in the work place. When our sexuality, be it our masculinity or our femininity, assigns us specific roles that have no bearing on our abilities, it becomes a limiting factor in our growth and development.

Family Lifestyles

Our expectations for family lifestyles are closely related to our image of appropriate male/female roles. If all women act one way and all men act another way, then relationships within the family as well as the behavior of specific family members are linked with these male/female images.

In addition, when man's work was in the world, parenting became the domain of the mother. Today some family life experts believe that despite the attention given to shared parenting, less parenting takes place when the mother is employed outside the home. Husbands have not assumed an equal share of household tasks even when the wife is working outside the home; neither have husbands taken on an equal share of the parenting role.

Whether it is because of nature or nurture, women in the traditional housewife role have provided a centering point for family members, all of whom need a "place to come home to." When we think that only women can perform this role or that the role is inferior, it is difficult to uncover its possibilities for teaching us how to respond to a deeply human need.

Sex Education

Sex education is more than passing on the mechanics of sex, though even doing this is affected by a person's sense of his/her own sexual identity. Actually sex education, education about what it means to be a male and a female, begins as soon as an infant is born. Sexual identity is formed in the early years of life. Role models are the adults encountered during those years.

Those of us who are adults often think we have performed our role as sex educator when we give our young people what one educator calls the "organ recital." As things stand, based on research done by the Committee on

Human Sexual Development, very few parents—even those who consider themselves sexually liberated—do an adequate job of giving information about the mechanics of sex. Discomfort about sexual activity translates into poor performance as sex educator. And poor sexual identity or failure to realize that sexuality is more than sex makes it difficult to convey a positive vision of sexuality to the next generation.

Erotic Behavior

The strong sexual attraction which assured the survival of our species is the most obvious and pressing manifestation of our sexuality. Though it is not the only manifestation, it is the one that receives the most attention. When the word "sexuality" is mentioned, the first thought that seems to spring into a person's mind is erotic sex. Since erotic behavior can be either pleasurable or destructive, people tend to have mixed reactions to the mention of sexual activity.

Through the ages erotic behavior has assumed a negative public image. Under the heading "Erotic Art" in the card catalogue at the University of Chicago Library many of the early entries have been changed from the category "Immoral Art." The equating of immoral and erotic also manifests itself in the laws—both civil and religious—regulating erotic behavior. Indeed, as was noted earlier, much of the focus of church statements, civil rules, and secular discussions of sexuality deal with erotic behavior, most often referred to as "sex."

Our obsession with sex is really our obsession with what is the correct erotic behavior, given our understanding of the reasons for this behavior. Negative attitudes about erotic behavior continue to thrive, even in a society whose members imagine themselves to be sexually liberated.

While one day we find our desire a positive influence in deepening a relationship, a few days later we regret that the attractiveness of another person intrudes into our well-ordered life. Confusion about the goal of erotic activity makes it difficult to discuss our opinions with a sexual partner or a potential sexual partner. Sexual desire often seems to betray us, offering the hope of a unity that seems impossible to attain.

Erotic activity—that is, sex—occupies our minds even when we are not engaging in it. Thus the feeling that we are obsessed with sex. At the same time we are fearful of the consequences of our erotic behavior: What demands will be placed on us? What demands can we place on another? While in our fantasy life we might imagine ourselves to have complete freedom to exercise our sexual desire, reality reminds us that we must have some degree of cooperation from the person we desire. Sexual desire is a constant reminder of the need to understand the meaning of our bodies with their sexuality.

Reproduction

While no one would argue against the claim that our reproductive capability is related to our sexuality, reproduction no longer is the only, or in most cases the primary, focus of discussions on sexuality in today's technological world. Yet, the reproductive capacity of our earliest ancestors has influenced the human personality.

Psychological maturity in an adult requires a concern

for the next generation. Erik Erickson's stages of growth and development indicate that once a person has solved her/his identity crisis s/he looks for someone with whom to share this identity and then they together become generative people, caring about the world beyond them in both space and time.

Even now most adults have a concrete manifestation of this generativity in their own children. People might not have as many children as they did in previous generations, but they invest a great deal of emotional energy into the care of those they have, perhaps expending more energy on two children than their ancestors did on eight or ten.

Also, the relationship between our sexual behavior and our reproduction, between our masculinity and our femininity, is being questioned as technological advances are making artificial insemination, frozen sperm, frozen embryos, *in vitro* fertilization, and surrogate motherhood realities, and test tube wombs have become a goal of some scientists. So, while sexuality is more than sex and more than reproduction, both sex and reproduction issues are constant reminders of the questions raised by our sexuality.

In concluding this overview of the situation of human sexuality, we can't help but wonder why it is that the human sexuality that was responsible for the survival of the species and that offers humankind the opportunity for the emotional bonding so crucial for growth in intimacy has also been a source of confusion throughout human history. What is there about sexuality that makes it so fearful? Why is it that both church and civil leaders have issued such dire warnings about the demonic possibilities of sex-

uality? Indeed, why have we humans let sexuality's demonic power be so predominant in our cultures? While
sexuality is, as we have seen, more than just sex, why has it
been difficult for humans to appreciate this more?

For our purpose here—developing contemporary Catholic guidelines on sexuality—we will suggest that the
answer to that why is closely linked with the emphasis on
the differences between men and women, differences that
have overshadowed their similarities, and differences that
though powerfully attractive are also threatening to our
desire for independence. In addition, in the male-domi-
nated culture of the church, the threat posed by the attractiveness of women made sexual desire an instinct to be controlled.

As we study the church's history and tradition we will
see that anti-sex ideas are closely linked to an anti-woman
mentality, a mentality that survives among many church
leaders even today. We will also see that a correct interpretation of Catholic doctrine must reject this anti-woman
and anti-sex attitude since it is heretical. Guidelines for a
Catholic understanding of sexuality must begin within an
identification of how this heresy took root and concentrate
on how to eliminate its hold on the church's teachings
about sexuality.

CHAPTER II
A Biblical View of Sexuality

What is seen with the eyes of the creator is masculine, and not feminine, for God does not stoop to look upon what is feminine and of the flesh.

Origen

Original unity . . . is based on masculinity and femininity, as if on two different "incarnations," that is, on two ways of "being a body" of the same human being, created "in the Image of God."

Pope John Paul II, Nov. 7, 1979

FOR many Catholics the final proof of the moral acceptability of an activity or an attitude is whether the Bible endorses or condemns it. Some Catholics adhere to a strict, literal interpretation of the Bible on sexuality-related matters. For example, according to this view, if St. Paul says wives should be subject to their husbands who are their heads just as Christ is the head of the church, then obviously women are inferior to men and should not aspire to activities that are part of men's work.

One problem with this literal interpretation of every verse of the Bible is that the Bible is a collection of various books addressed to different audiences over many generations and with many contradictory statements. Contradic-

tory attitudes on sexuality exist even within the letters of
St. Paul.

An even greater problem occurs when the Bible is treated
as a textbook of social ethics or as a sourcebook to be con-
sulted for specific answers about modern sexual issues.
Many of our questions regarding correct sexual behavior
were not even considered in the biblical period. The sexual
practices allowed or forbidden in that time are related to
the economic and social conditions which varied during the
more than thousand years of biblical history.

It is not enough to consider only the prohibitions of the
biblical period in a search for the Bible's views on sexuality. Other questions to consider are: what is the predominant attitude on sexuality throughout the Bible; and what,
if any, other themes emerge from an analysis of biblical
situations? "What the Bible says" is an interpretation of
what is in the Bible, an interpretation that often takes an
idea out of context and uses it to support a particular, pre-
conceived view. Interpretation of the biblical views with no
reference to their context generally results in misrepresen-
tation of the Catholic perspective on sexuality.

Literary and historical criticism emphasize the historical
context and the literary character of a law, saying, story, or
teaching. The final criterion in this analysis must be
whether the interpretation agrees with the basic beliefs of
the faith or contradicts these tenets. For example, any biblical situation that is interpreted to mean that the body or
sexuality is intrinsically evil is contrary to the uniquely
Catholic understanding of the sacramentality of creation—
Yahweh looked upon all that He had created and saw that
it was good.

Since much of the past and even the present official Catholic attitude on sexuality is based on interpretation of biblical matter, guidelines for discovering a Catholic perspective must review at least some of the biblical material that has been used to support this attitude.

At one level the church has been, and in some instances continues to be, negative in its interpretation of a biblical view of sexuality, at times using a literal interpretation of biblical texts, often taken out of their context. More than likely, Origen would have considered the fact that "God created man in the image of himself" proof for his belief that what God looked upon and saw as "good" was masculine, leading to the view expressed in his quote at the beginning of this chapter.

Still, there are many instances where negative views on sexuality are present in the Bible. In those cases, an analysis of the cultural context of the biblical view often makes it obvious that the biblical statement is heavily influenced by this context. In other instances, especially when the biblical view is compared to other attitudes of the same period, we discover a minor, but significant, positive attitude about sexuality often existing alongside of the negative view.

Since the Bible itself, as well as the sexual views based on an interpretation of the Bible, developed in cultures with a strong anti-woman bias and with limited scientific understanding of sexuality, a review of biblical attitudes on both women and sex as well as examination of the various prohibitions and directives regarding proper sexual behavior are necessary. Biblical law and biblical "literature"— stories, poetry, prayers—provide insights into the attitudes of both the Old and New Testament periods.

THE OLD TESTAMENT

The Law

Since laws generally deal with what is inadmissible in a society, they give us a sense of, if not the real problems, at least what lawmakers see as potential problems for the society. It is possible that some of the ancient Israelite laws governing sexual behavior were aimed at discouraging practices that flourished in surrounding cultures and that seemed anathema to the Israelite view of an ordered society with Yahweh as its God. For example, the notion of cultic purity with its emphasis on external cleanliness—including freedom from the impurity brought about by sexual discharge—is related to the mystery encountered in so much of ordinary experience. However, there also is the repeated command from Yahweh to avoid the evil ways of those who preceded them into the promised land and whose customs (especially many of their sexual practices) rendered them ritualistically impure.

Other laws responded to the importance of the patriarchal family structure and the need to assure the legitimacy of offspring. Reproduction and sexual behavior were the primary focus of the laws on sexuality in the Old Testament period.

Cultic Purity

The laws announced in both Leviticus and Deuteronomy show the importance of cultic purity for the Israelites and how, for them, physical sexuality was a source of ritual impurity.

Leviticus 12 described the rite of purification of a woman after childbirth. If she had a son, she was unclean until his circumcision on the eighth day. She then had to wait an additional 31 days for her blood to be purified before she could touch anything consecrated or go into the sanctuary. If she gave birth to a girl she was unclean for two weeks and had to wait 66 days for her blood to be purified.

Leviticus 15 spelled out the sexual impurities of men and women and how these contaminated those who came in contact with their discharges, plus details for the method of purification for each. Both men and women who had intercourse were unclean until the evening after the intercourse. Women were unclean for seven days after their monthly menstrual period; on the eighth day they had to submit to a purification ritual of atonement. And any man who slept with a woman during her period would also be unclean for the same seven days, as would be anything or anyone either of them touched.

The Deuteronomic Code also emphasized the importance of sexual purity when it excluded castrated males and bastards from the assembly of Yahweh (23:2-4) and banished a man who had a nocturnal emission from camp until sunset when, after washing himself, he could be readmitted. In addition, it forbade incest and intercourse with an animal, placing a curse on those who engaged in such behavior.

Patriarchal Family Structures

Again we turn to Leviticus and Deuteronomy for a review of the laws about sexual behavior that were supportive of the family structure. Conjugal regulations as well as rules for all sorts of sexual behavior are covered in these two books.

Leviticus 18 warned against the customs of the unbelieving Canaanites. Sons of Israel were not to practice incest, have intercourse with a menstruating woman, lie with a man or an animal, or allow a woman to lie with an animal.

Leviticus 19 detailed what a man must do to obtain forgiveness for the sin of having intercourse with another man's concubine. Since she was not a free woman, he would not be put to death. Instead, he had to present a ram of reparation to the priest who then performed the rite of atonement over him.

Leviticus 20 outlined offenses against the family. In addition to those who sinned through false worship, those who had to die were: anyone who cursed his mother or father, committed adultery with a married woman or with his neighbor's wife (she too should die), or practiced any form of incest (with disastrous deaths, including the curse of childlessness). And if a man should lie with a woman during her period both he and she were to be outlawed. All of these activities were detrimental to the reproductive goal of sexual activity. They could render a man childless, the worst fate for an Israelite male.

According to Levite Law, women were to remain virgins until they married. Any deviation was a sin, punishable by death. Virginity in women at the time of marriage was prized because it assured the man that any offspring of the union were his children.

The directives in Deuteronomy 22 show the importance of virginity. If a husband suspected his bride was not a virgin and charged her with this offense, her parents had to prove to the elders (males) of the city that she was a virgin. If the elders were convinced by the parents' arguments, the husband was whipped. He also had to pay a fine to the father of the bride, who then returned the bride to her husband who must not ever put her away again. If the parents could not prove their daughter's virginity, they were to bring her to her father's door where the men of the city would stone her to death because she had played the harlot in her father's house bringing folly into Israel. In both instances the father of the bride is the one who was insulted.

Deuteronomy 22 also dealt with punishments for rape. If the rape was of a betrothed virgin, the punishment depended on location. If she had been raped in the city, they were both to be stoned to death—she because she could have cried out for help; he because he had violated the wife of a fellow man. If the rape occurred in the country where help would not have been available, only the man was to die, because he had violated her. If the virgin was unbetrothed, the man had to pay her father a fine, marry her, and not ever divorce her.

Adultery was also heinous according to the law, though there were exceptions for a man. Still, according to the law, if a man had intercourse with a married woman, the penalty for both was death. However, if an unmarried woman had intercourse with a married man, the man was not punished.

Deuteronomy 24 outlined the provisions for the writ of divorce, available to the man only. If he was displeased with his wife or found some impropriety in her, a man could make out a writ of divorce, hand it to her and dismiss her from his house. However, if she married again and was similarly dismissed or was widowed, her first husband could not take her back.

A final example of the importance of reproduction in the Israelite family is found in the levirate law presented in Deuteronomy 25. If the man died childless, his brother who was living with him had to marry his wife; and the first child of this union was to be named after the deceased man. If the brother refused, a ritual is outlined that made his refusal public knowledge; from then on he had to bear an uncomplimentary epithet. However, the surviving brother still became sole owner of the house and property which he had jointly owned before his brother's death.

In summary, the laws of ancient Israel sought to control the demonic possibilities seen lurking in sexual desire in order to assure the greater good of the society. In addition, the idea that association with anything related to physical sexuality made one unworthy of participation in the cult, seems to indicate a certain distaste for sexuality. But since there were many other practices that rendered a person impure, the directives regarding sexual impurities must be considered in light of the understandings of an ancient semi-nomadic people who felt that any human imperfections were not worthy of their God. Irregular sexual behavior was viewed as an imperfection, and since natural sexual functions (menstruation, childbirth, intercourse, semen) were somehow linked to this imperfection, they too were suspect.

The law acknowledged the necessity of sexuality, but there is little sense of joy exhibited in the way the law discusses sexuality. Perhaps this is inevitable, given the nature of law. It is a drawback of the religions' emphasis on law and morality when they examine the mystery of human sexuality.

The laws that related to the importance of the family structure do not seem to be as anti-sex as they are anti-woman. Woman was little more than a possession of a man: first of all, of her father; in the event of his death, of her brothers; and then finally of her husband who had been chosen by her brothers or father. She was forced to marry a man who raped her, and was stoned to death if her husband claimed she was not a virgin or if she was raped while betrothed and unable to get help when she cried out.

LITERATURE

Laws give a limited, legal view of a society's attitude about sexuality. The stories, the poetry, the hymns (poetry for ritual) and the images of God of a community tell about the "imagination" of the society. The tales of the life of Yahweh's people reveal the Israelites' original vision of sexuality, how difficult it was for the community to live out this vision, how stereotypes limited the possibility of personhood for women, and yet how a positive view of sexuality managed to be affirmed periodically in the community.

In particular, the creation and fall story in Genesis, the prophets Isaiah, Hosea, and Ezekiel in their presentation of Yahweh as a spouse, the condemnations of the Baal worshipers, the practice of concubinage, the practice of the writ of divorce, the portrayal of women—including the Wisdom Literature's praises and condemnations of her—

and the erotic love poetry of the Song of Songs all contribute to a mixed attitude about sexuality.

A brief review of the vision, the attitudes towards women, and the Song of Songs show both a positive and a negative appreciation of sexuality. Unfortunately, the negative exercised the greater influence, even when the positive was more true to the biblical affirmation of allegiance to Yahweh.

The Vision

Genesis 2 and 3 are evidence that the ancient writers of the Old Testament recognized God's hand in the creation of sexuality and humankind's rejection of God's gift. Genesis 2:18-25, especially when linked to the later and more "theological" Genesis 1:26-31, makes it clear that human sexuality was for the Israelite, as it is for us, a mystery.

The story suggests that although the male/female relationship, including that of sexual intimacy, was generally experienced as one of opposition (a result of the fall—Genesis 3), there were times when it was felt to be the occasion of joy—similar to the discovery of another who was "bone of my bones and flesh of my flesh." When this discovery led to "clinging together to become one flesh," the partners had no reason to fear their nakedness (Genesis 2:23-25).

In the ordered environment of Eden, sexuality was always like the very best male/female relationship, one in which the partners discovered their unique place in Yahweh's plan, where each was special, each was "good."

After the fall, sexuality became disordered and the relationship became distorted; man and woman were at odds, afraid of their nakedness.

Attitudes Towards Women

Whether or not the Genesis author meant the order of human creation (Adam first, and then Eve from his side) to indicate male superiority or to blame Eve for the fall of humankind, these interpretations of creation and of the fall have contributed to a rationalization of the acceptance of women as inferior. This attitude predominates in the imagination of the Old Testament, with some significant exceptions.

Stories of concubinage (Genesis 30:1-13), of women offered as sexual lures to distract irate men from attacking foreign guests, and of women as harlots (even in the positive prophetic images of God as lover of Israel, Israel is presented as a faithless woman) are combined with denunciations of women who can, for example, cause drooping hands and weak knees when they don't make their husbands happy (Sirach 25:21-26). The link between a negative posture towards women and fear of the sexual drive is apparent when men are advised to avoid looking at an attractive woman because her beauty is misleading, exciting passion (Sirach 9:8-9).

In the book of Proverbs women were portrayed as predators and men as their innocent victims. The adulterous woman, the very opposite of the obedient wife, tempts men and inevitably will lead them to their death (Proverbs 6:29, 7:4-13, 18-19, 21-23, 25-27). Though woman is often portrayed as little more than a sex object, she is a sex object of which men should be leery, never trusting her completely.

There were "exceptional" women in the Bible, women who stood out, not just as the Perfect Wife (Proverbs 31:10-31), but in contrast to the stereotype of the subservient woman. A list of the "exceptional" women in the Old Testament would include: Deborah, a judge and prophetess; Jael, the slayer of an evil Canaanite captain (Judges 4 & 5); Athaliah, who ruled Israel for six years (2 Kings 11:1-3); and Chuldah, the prophetess (2 Kings 22:16-17). However, the numbers of these women are few; and in many of their tales it is their sexual attractiveness that causes death to the enemy. There clearly was an ambivalence toward this attractiveness as a positive, unifying tool.

One definite positive image of woman emerges in Isaiah, where God is portrayed as a Mother (Isaiah 42:13-14; 49:14-15; 66:12-13). If woman's experience was used to describe God, then women ought to have been considered in a more favorable light than generally was presented in the Old Testament.

The Song of Songs

There has been much discussion about this erotic love poem and the significance of its presence in the Bible. Is it merely a secular poem, celebrating the joys and sorrows of erotic love? Was it meant to be a representation of the relationship between Yahweh and Israel? Was it allegorical? Was it borrowed from another culture? Questions such as these have plagued biblical scholars in the past and continue to do so even now.

Whatever interpretation is given to the poem, its erotic imagery cannot be denied. The lover and his beloved fantasize about eventual sexual union. They rejoice in the physical attractiveness they see in each other. They are sad when they are apart and happy when they are together. Although the female voice predominates (leading some to attribute its authorship to women), both the man and the woman articulate a desire to be in the presence of the other.

An equality of persons emerges from this imagery. Perhaps because of this equality, this recognition of the personhood of woman, the poem is able to treat sexual desire as the unifying force described in Genesis 2. Obviously some individuals within the Israelite community had come to appreciate this possibility, despite the more negative attitude that portrayed stereotypic roles and saw reproduction as the only end of sex for a woman and as the primary sexual goal of the community.

THE NEW TESTAMENT

The New Testament is even less of a sourcebook for answers to specific sexual morality statements. Jesus was not a law maker. Rather, he was a vision giver. He came to fulfill the law by moving beyond the law. He offered people an opportunity to participate in God's plan for life, an exciting plan, but one that easily was forgotten without the help of the Spirit. He did not focus on sexual morality, but his vision of life suggests an appreciation of sexuality that goes beyond one that can be gained by following rules.

So it is not surprising that the Gospel and epistle writers, many of whom expected the second coming in their lifetime, did not address issues of sexual behavior in a systematic way. Still, both the Gospels and the epistles reflect some startling ideas on sexuality. As recent feminist biblical scholarship shows, there was a certain audacity in the roles women played in the early church, an audacity that was curbed due to a fear of increased animosity from the surrounding cultures and that was unable to regain a foothold in successive Christian communities.

The Gospels

The Gospel accounts of the Good News were addressed to specific religious communities. The life of Jesus was redacted—oral stories were gathered together—with these various audiences in mind. Since the emphasis in each Gospel was to help build the faith of the audience, specific religious concerns of a community often dictated the focus of the story.

What stands out in all the Gospels, however, is the attitude of Jesus toward the women around him. Though those who claim Jesus was a feminist are attributing to the Gospel story-tellers ideas that were not even considered by the Gospel writers or by Jesus, his attitude toward women was revolutionary. He associated with women (Luke 8:2); used their experiences in his parables (Matthew 13:33; Luke 7:11-19); took pity on them (Mark 1:29-31; Luke 7:11-19); and appeared to them before anyone else after his resurrection, letting them spread the word of his return to the disciples (Matthew 28:1-10; Mark 16:1-8; Luke 24:1-11; John 20:1-18).

A second important attitude of Jesus is apparent when, in addressing the specific issues of divorce and adultery, he moves beyond the "law" understanding found in the Old Testament. Divorce is wrong because it goes against the reasons for sexuality found "in the beginning" (Matthew 19:3-8). Although adultery is condemned, even looking at a woman lustfully is committing "adultery in the heart." The key words here are "looking lustfully," which most interpreters have taken as a condemnation of erotic fantasies, but which some recent interpretations have seen as a disregard for the dignity, the personhood of a woman.

Jesus turned the world of those whom he encountered upside down with his parables and with the parable of his actions. His treatment of women and his emphasis on sexual behavior's being evaluated according to its adherence to the image presented "in the beginning" are examples of the disruption of accepted attitudes that he caused.

The Epistles

St. Paul is the biblical authority most often quoted for support of notions on women and on sex. Few people would attempt to argue that Paul was a feminist. Save for his famous pronouncement that there is no difference between male and female (Galatians 3:28), his views are not immediately supportive of a positive view of sexuality.

1 Corinthians 7 contains his ideas on marriage and virginity, the theme of which is that since sex is always a danger, people should marry. He has been excused for this anti-sex mentality by his expectation that the Parousia was imminent and that nothing should distract the Christian from preparing for it. He was not issuing a directive to be adhered to by later generations since he did not expect there to be such a time.

Yet, St. Paul is not completely consistent in his views about sexuality. In another place he compares the relationship between a man and a woman to that of Christ and the church, referring back to Genesis 2:24 and laying the groundwork for considering marriage a sacrament. But in this same exhortation he recommends that women should regard their husbands as they regard the Lord (Ephesians 5:21-33). Furthermore, wives were to be subject to their husbands, who were to love them and not be harsh to them (Colossians 3:18).

St. Paul's views on sexual desire might have sprung from the attitude he expressed in his comments on women. Women were to remain silent in church. Any questions they had they could address to their husbands at home (1 Corinthians 14:34). They were to keep their heads covered to avoid distractions; but men, who were the image and glory of God, were not to cover their heads. In addition, man was not created for woman, but woman was created for man (so, too, woman was made from man, while man was not made from woman) (1 Corinthians); and women should be submissive and not teach (1 Timothy:2). Even if it was not his intention to establish a sexual ethic for the future church, St. Paul supplied the basis for many future negative pronouncements on both sex and women.

Still, there are indications that there was an initial attempt in the early Christian Church to follow through on the idea that there was neither male nor female. Women were called co-heirs in the life of grace (1 Peter 3:7). They also were active in the New Testament communities as deaconesses (Romans 16:1), instructors (Acts 18:26), and charitable workers (Acts 9:36), even establishing "house churches" (Philemon 2; 1 Corinthians 16:19; Romans 16:

3-5; Acts 16:14; Colossians 4:15). And women were con-
spicuous in Paul's missionary movement (1 Thessalonians
5:12; Philippians 4:2; 1 Corinthians 9:5; Romans 16:1ff),
often almost equal in number to the men in a particular
mission (Romans 16).

In summary, we see that the New Testament, like the
Old Testament, presents an ambivalent "imagination" regarding sexuality. While rejecting the cultic purity taboos
of the Jewish culture from which it sprang and allowing
women active participation in the life of the community
which indicated a position of equality in God's eyes, the
New Testament communities also continued some negative
perceptions of women that flourished in the cultures in
which they developed. Unfortunately, these negative
perceptions have been the accepted wisdom of the New
Testament for many who regard sex as evil and women as
the source of this evil.

As we attempt to develop guidelines for a Catholic perspective on sexuality, we need to keep in mind that both
the Old and New Testament understandings of creation
suggest a vision of sexuality as sacramental. Even if this
vision did not develop in the patriarchal cultures of those
eras, the basis for the vision remains as an important contribution to a Catholic discussion of the meaning of sexuality.

Although Jesus can be said to have acknowledged the
goodness of sexuality and to have exhibited a regard for
women that should have encouraged the idea of sex as
sacramental to flourish, the threats from the surrounding
cultures supported contrary views. The positive perspective
promoted by Jesus lost out and has yet to regain its rightful
place in a Christian interpretation of sexuality.

PART TWO

CHAPTER III
Sexuality in the Church Tradition

There are three evils in the world: water, fire and woman. However, though water may drown you, it also sustains your life; so too, fire that can burn you also keeps you warm and cooks your food; therefore, neither of these are intrinsically evil. But even to look upon a woman can cause your arousal; therefore woman is intrinsically evil.

> Paraphrase of advice from an anonymous medieval Italian monk

The primary end of marriage is the procreation and nurture of children; its secondary end is mutual help and the remedying of concupiscence.

> Canon 1013, CODE OF CANON LAW, 1917

IN the eighteen hundred plus years between the end of the New Testament period and the beginning of the Second Vatican Council the church's teachings on sexuality have continued to reflect the ambivalence established in the biblical period. The world to which the church spread had concerns not all that unlike those of ancient Israel and the early Christian communities: societies were patriarchal; survival—both individual and communal—was of paramount interest; reproduction was decreed by economic needs; men were the principal rulers, thinkers, educators,

warriors, and religious leaders; women were defined by their anatomy and judged to be inferior even when there was evidence that there were alternative possibilities. And though the world changed over the centuries, ideas about sexuality both in the church and in the secular world continued to be influenced by the views of these earlier societies.

Theological statements, church laws, sacramental procedures, ritual requirements, and conciliar pronouncements abound, reflecting the official church's stand on sexuality-related matters during its long history. Like the biblical religious leaders that preceded them, church leaders exhibited a strong negative attitude on issues dealing with sex and women, while at the same time often ignoring the implications of some of the doctrinal beliefs that might have led them to other conclusions. Although it is possible to find a number of positive ideas among these documents, the general impression is that church leaders have not been disposed to speak favorably about human sexuality. Some proponents of an understanding of sexuality based on the Tradition often use these resources as the *only* basis for understanding "what the church teaches" about sexuality.

At an unofficial level, the believing faithful were influenced by the negative views on women and sexuality that are part of any patriarchal society. Still, there are traces of an "imagination" on sexuality issues that was more in keeping with the positive possibilities found in the story of creation, the Song of Songs, the position of Jesus, and the claim that there is no difference between male and female in the new order brought by Christ. This unofficial "imagination," it must be admitted, was a minor strain within the Catholic tradition.

We need to review the official church's position regarding marriage, sex, and women during three periods (Patristic, Middle Ages, and post-Reformation) in order to gain an overview of what the Tradition (official) taught about sexuality. We also will investigate attitudes toward women in the unofficial church during these same periods to show how the tradition (small "t") kept alive the possibility of woman as person. Without this concept a positive vision of sexuality, using Genesis 2 as a guideline, could not be developed. In addition, we will examine how rituals and reflections on the femininity of God contributed to an "imagination" that could see the positive, sacramental possibilities of sexuality.

Both avenues of investigation (tradition with a capital and with a small "t") reveal a more complex response to the mystery of human sexuality than that which is presented with the assurance that "The church has *always* taught in this manner."

THE TRADITION (CAPITAL "T")

The Patristic Era (Second to Fifth Century)

As with previous religious thinkers, the Fathers of the Church were influenced by the culture in which they lived. Their ideas on sexuality were both affected by and a response to the excesses of the religious and pagan philosophical thought of their day. Their views on sexuality, expounded in response to the "false" ideas of the time, also reflect how pervasive an influence these ideas had, even on the Fathers themselves.

Many of these early church thinkers were presenting alternatives to Gnosticism with its pessimistic view of life. According to this world view, evil and goodness were co-equal components of the universe. The spiritual was the good element of the universe while the material element was evil. Since sexuality was material, it was, by its very nature, evil. Indulgence in sexually related behavior was morally evil.

Two different lifestyles flowed from this understanding of the universe: one, a rigorous asceticism; the other, a wild antinomianism. Attitudes on sex and marriage differed in these two groups. The ascetic condemned marriage as an invention of the evil deity. The libertines claimed that they had been freed from obsolete laws and therefore any sexual behavior was acceptable; indeed, sexual freedom was to be practiced by those who wanted to imitate the divine ideal.

In addition, the Fathers' thought shows the influence of Philo, who taught a sharp dualism between body and soul. For him it was a moral requirement that people free themselves of the body with its sensate elements. The Stoic ideal of virtue and antipathy toward human passions was a secular response to the excesses of the time.

Ideas on virginity and celibacy as primary Christian values, along with the notion of marriage as sacramental, also helped shape many of the reflections during this period. As the church became more institutional, legislation for all areas of life, including the sexual, began to appear. The Fathers' attitude on women might help explain why they failed to develop a deeper appreciation of sexuality.

Ideas on Sex

The dominant attitude toward physical sexuality was negative. At one time or the other, the sex act was called filthy, degrading, unseemly, unclean, shameful, and a defilement by the Church Fathers. Clement of Alexandria, Irenaeus, and Tertullian were among those who engaged in a dual struggle against the Gnostics. They were in opposition to the exaggerated asceticism that rejected all sexuality, while at the same time they were challenged by the antinomians to look for a meaning of sexuality that kept it within marriage.

Gregory of Nyssa, John Chrysostom, Jerome, and Augustine all saw sex as separate from love. Sex with its carnal desire, irrational behavior and pleasure obviously was sinful. Jerome went so far as to declare that a husband was guilty of sin if he had intercourse with his wife in such a way that, even if she were not his wife, he would have wanted to possess her.

Virginity was superior to marriage because it rejected sexual activity. Marriage was for the weaker, ordinary person. Even then, those who were too weak to practice celibacy—who did marry—were encouraged to seek for the ideal passionless intercourse of the Garden when they acted to reproduce themselves. From this perspective sexual abstinence was as much an ideal after marriage as it was before marriage.

The conjugal act was legitimate, honorable, a duty; but only when it was directed toward its naturally ordered end. For this reason, couples were forbidden to have intercourse when a woman was already pregnant. This prohibition was included along with those against sodomy, bestiality, fornication and adultery in a collection of disciplinary canons. All these activities were unnatural, that is, they were not used for reproductive purposes.

According to Augustine, who set the stage for much of the later thinking on sexuality, the fault of sexual sin was not with God but with Adam and Eve. There had been no concupiscence in the Garden, no eroticism, no ecstasy. After the fall, concupiscence made Adam and Eve aware of their nakedness, and the guilt of that original sin continued. Every child born of the necessarily evil act of intercourse was born into sin.

Augustine was reacting against the Manicheans who saw sexual desire and procreation as essentially evil. He defended the goodness of procreative sexuality but saw concupiscence as the consequence of the fall.

Marriage

A review of the doctrine of marriage as it evolved during this period reveals much about what the Fathers saw as the meaning of sexuality. The early Fathers used the natural law argument borrowed from the Stoics against Gnostic extremes. This allowed them to defend marriage, justifying it with procreation and excluding bodily love and sexual desire. In the final analysis it seems that only procreation and the need to avoid a greater sin justified marriage.

Gregory of Nyssa taught that the innocence before the fall was like that of the angels who did not need sexual intercourse. Therefore, if humankind had not fallen there would have been no need for marriage; there would have been another way of propagating the human race. John

Chrysostom thought the same, but also felt that marriage allowed men and women an outlet for lustful sexual desire. Since God did not need marriage to propagate, marriage was inferior. Justin Martyr claimed that Christians who married should do so with only one thought, to have children; otherwise they should forego marriage and remain chaste.

Clement of Alexandria maintained that a man must exclude goals other than procreation from an act of intercourse. A man loved his wife only if he sought to have a child by her, not if he only joined with her out of sexual desire. Men were told they must practice continence in marriage. However, Clement did not view marriage as narrowly as Justin Martyr. He saw value in the mutual support and love of the partners which formed an external bond.

Ambrose explained why Elizabeth was embarrassed by conceiving a child: the elderly were not supposed to have intercourse, since they were beyond the possibility of conceiving. And, according to Jerome, if intercourse was not for conception only, it was filthy and lustful.

In Augustine's opinion, intercourse was without sin only in marriage and only if it was specifically accompanied by a desire for conception. Otherwise, if the intention was pleasure, or if pleasure was enjoyed, it was a venial sin; if it was with other than a spouse or if it was done in a way so as to avoid conception, it was a mortal sin. Also, only the good of procreation rescued carnal concupiscence; therefore, sterility rendered intercourse sinful.

Augustine insisted, against the Manichees, that marriage since the fall was not fundamentally evil. Against the Pelagian charge that he was too close to Manicheanism, he defended the fundamental goodness of marriage at the beginning. He saw the good of marriage in its end, children; in its law, the mutual fidelity of the spouses; and in its sacramental power, the indissoluble union between husband and wife. Fidelity meant honoring the other's exclusive right to sexual partnership. All remarriage was adultery.

Marriage was a sacrament, according to Augustine, in so far as it signaled a comparison of the union between man and woman with that of Christ and the church. This idea of sacrament was used as the rationale for the indissolubility of marriage, but it was not a sacrament like baptism, making participants members of the Body of Christ. Tertullian and Cyprian also used the word "sacramentum" in reference to marriage; but for them, too, it was not sacrament in the later technical definition of the word as a participation in the life of Christ.

For these thinkers, Christian marriage was superior to that of pagans because it was a sign of Christ and church. Jerome reminded couples that their relations should be holy because their marriage was holy. Still, there was discussion of the possibility that even pagan marriages were sacramental because these marriages were a sign of commitment.

In addition to this rudimentary theology of marriage enunciated by the Fathers, the church was also developing a discipline of marriage. This discipline began to evolve as the church became more institutionalized. For example, Ignatius of Antioch taught that the bishop ought to preside at marriages between Christians. Widows and widowers could remarry, though this was not the ideal. And slaves could enter a valid marriage. By the time of St. Augustine, impediments to a valid marriage existed; and there was a practice of penalties for marriages that did not adhere to the laws of unity and indissolubility.

Divorce was an area where the Fathers had divided opinions. According to St. Jerome, even if a husband was an adulterer, or a sodomite, or a hardened criminal who had been left because of his crimes, he was still the husband and his wife could not remarry while he lived. But Origen, Basil, and John Chrysostom held that the husband who was victimized by divorce was allowed to remarry. This latter position eventually developed into the tradition of the Eastern church, which allows the injured person to remarry.

The discussion of marriage and sexuality by the Fathers was the first step in the development of a Tradition on these subjects. St. Augustine's "goods" of marriage occupy a prominent position in later church discussions on marriage and sexuality. So, too, the church as marriage legislator was to have enormous influence in the future discussions of the meaning of sexuality.

Women

A reading of the Fathers' ideas on women suggests that they were continuing the anti-woman attitude of the patriarchal culture. More than likely, woman's experience was never seen as important for their reflections on sexuality. Tertullian thought of women as "the devil's gateway." Clement of Alexandria saw women as man's equal in everything, but man as better than women at everything.

He also prohibited women from participation in the
physical sports of wrestling and running, since the Bible indicated they should confine their activities to spinning,
weaving, and cooking. Jerome wanted women to avoid
washing themselves so as to decrease their attractiveness.

St. John Chrysostom maintained that since woman
taught once and ruined everything (the Fall), she should
not be allowed to teach again. And St. Augustine claimed
that man, not woman, was made in the image of God,
making woman incomplete without man, but man complete without woman.

In summary, the Fathers of the Church and the church
in the patristic era were suspicious of sexuality. Sexual
desire and the pleasure of sexual union were tainted and
could only be made acceptable if there was a good end—
procreation. Women were not accorded full personhood.
In an attempt to deny the condemnation of marriage and
sex by the ascetics and at the same time to restrain the antinomians, the Fathers turned to the natural philosophy of
the pagans. By so doing they distanced themselves from
the vitality of the vision reiterated by Jesus.

The Middle Ages

The Middle Ages inherited the ideas on sexuality of the
Patristic period, and church thinkers either defended these
ideas over against contrary practices of their day or
evolved new understandings based on situations that were
more apparent to them than they had been to those in the
earlier period. Especially important in understanding the
medieval approach to sexuality are the penitentials of the

early Middle Ages, the ongoing canonical discussions on what makes a marriage—consent or the first act of intercourse—and St. Thomas Aquinas' teaching on sex and marriage. In addition, the overall attitude toward women during this period again indicates why reflections on sexuality seldom took their experience into consideration.

The Penitentials

The penitentials were guidebooks for confessors containing specific penances for various offenses. As far as sex was concerned, the penitentials reflected the view that only marital sex was allowed and then only with the thought of children. However, knowing the temptations of sexual desire, the penitentials indicated penances for every variant of sex that was not heterosexual, oriented toward conception, and between man and wife with the man in the superior position (the only "natural" position for intercourse).

The penitentials were regionally compiled and reflected a wide knowledge of sexual deviations. The major sex sin was contraception, with penances varying according to circumstances but consisting of fasts ranging between three and fifteen years. Penances for masturbation, homosexuality, and abortion also varied according to circumstances.

The fasts usually consisted of abstinence from food and drink or from sex or some other self-indulgence. Beginning in the eleventh century self-flagellation (for the religious) and whipping of the laity by the parish priest were introduced. Singing of penitential psalms was sometimes demanded. For example, a man who had nocturnal emissions was required to rise immediately and sing several psalms.

The penitentials of the early Middle Ages mirrored the thinking of men like Gregory the Great and Caesarius of Arles. Gregory, who was pope from 590 to 604, saw sexual desire as the punishment for sin. Since the sexual appetite came from the first sin, no one is born into the world without this sin. Married couples always sinned when they had intercourse, because there was sexual pleasure in their intercourse. Caesarius, Bishop of Arles in the sixth century, spoke out against the fornication and other sexual disorders brought about by the barbarian invasions. He maintained that all sexual relationships were sinful.

Peter Lombard reiterated Augustine's teaching that intercourse was evil if it was engaged in for any purpose other than procreation. He, too, believed that concupiscence leads to the act of generation, which in turn transmits original sin.

Canonical Discussions of Marriage

Disputes over marriage during the Middle Ages revolved around questions over what constituted a valid, indissoluble marriage. Was it, as the Roman law held, the mutual consent of the bride and groom? Or was it, as the Germanic tradition maintained, the act of intercourse? The debate that ensued in defense of both positions had a significant impact on the Catholic understanding of marriage. The juridical understanding of the indissolubility of a valid, consummated, and therefore sacramental marriage evolved from this debate. Marriage as contract has dominated Catholic marriage reflection until the most recent

past, when the idea of marriage as ongoing covenant began
to be enunciated.

Sex and Marriage in the Scholastic Tradition

In the twelfth century and early thirteenth century the
Albigensians and the Cathars became the heretics whose
ideas on sex and marriage had to be refuted by the theologians of the day. The heresy of these groups started with
the belief that every pleasure of the flesh was sinful, making marriage naturally sinful because it was a carnal bond.
And the consequence of this sin was even greater: an act of
conception dragged a soul, happy in God's presence, down
into the sinfulness of the flesh.

Over against these heresies, Thomas Aquinas defined
marriage as "a certain joining together of husband and
wife ordained to carnal intercourse and a further conse-
quent union between husband and wife." He based his
definition on what he saw as the "nature" of marriage and
sex. However, he had some suspicion about the power of
sexual passion when it could drive out reason.

Other thinkers taught as the Fathers had done—sex was
allowed only in marriage, with children as its primary purpose. The anti-woman mentality of the age would not per-
mit them to see the possibility of a communion of persons
in which sexual union would be an aid to the bonding of
the partners.

Attitude Toward Women

There is a contradiction in Thomas Aquinas' thinking
about sexuality, a contradiction that might explain why he

was never able to imagine a vision of sexuality as sacramental, even though his belief in the natural goodness of sex should have led to that conclusion. In his view, woman, who was created from man's rib, was destined to have some social partnership with man, but this was limited to the biological partnership necessary for procreation. A man was a much better partner in other endeavors. Man, who had the "discretion of reason," was the natural head of the family. His superiority was demonstrated in the act of intercourse, where he took the active, noble role and the woman was passive and submissive. Thomas also thought that women's souls were defective forms of male souls. His thought was reflective of the general attitude of the thinkers of his time, who felt that women had little worth save as receptacles for the male seed, the active principle in conception.

Counter-Reformation

The nearly four hundred years between the Council of Trent and the Second Vatican Council began with serious reform and ended with the need for another serious reform. Throughout this period, the emphasis on sexuality continued to be on sexual sins and questions related to marriage.

"Morals manuals" replaced the penitentials as the guide to correct sexual behavior. These manuals reflected the continued emphasis on procreation, categorizing sexual sins according to whether they preserved the procreative function and were thus in accord with nature or whether they were contrary to nature because they interfered with the procreative process. "Natural," again, related to the physical side of sexuality. Sexuality continued to be viewed as erotic behavior and reproduction.

By the first half of the twentieth century there was rather widespread lessening of the harsh demand that procreation be the only justifiable reason for intercourse. However, artificial contraception was considered sinful. In 1930, in reaction to the Anglican bishops' decision at the Lambeth Conference to allow birth control when there were morally good reasons, Pope Pius XI issued *Casti Connubii,* condemning the practice. However, he admitted to the secondary ends of marriage (mutual aid, the cultivating of mutual love, and the quieting of concupiscence), and allowed the use of rhythm. His views were reaffirmed by Pope Pius XII in his "Address to the Midwives" in 1951.

Lacking any positive vision of sexuality and encouraged by clergy educated with the "marriage manuals," the laity in the period prior to Vatican II came to believe that sexual transgressions were the most grievous sins they could commit. Indeed, many people came to consider the true judge of someone's church membership to be his or her adherence to the laws of sexual morality. They were not unlike the Pharisees, looking for someone to confirm that the law was the right way to understand sexuality. The time was ripe for a Catholic vision of sexuality that would clear up the confusion people experienced when they began to question the laws that did not seem to make sense. Instead, as we will see, they got more emphasis on the law.

TRADITION WITH A SMALL "t"

While the scholars carried on their lively debates, talking with other scholars, the majority of the faithful lived in ignorance of the problems being debated. The anti-woman attitudes of the patriarchal cultures were certainly influential in the lives of the ordinary people, making it difficult for them to imagine a union of man and woman that would resemble the vision of Genesis 2; but the religious scholars' legitimization of these ideas was not always part of the experience of the faithful.

As we noted before, the union of persons of this vision could not be appreciated in a society that failed to recognize the personhood of woman. And, as we saw in our analysis of the Tradition of the church, there was little appreciation of woman or woman's experience in these reflections. So we must turn to the less well known tradition and study what women were doing that might give the lie to the claim of their inferiority.

Recent feminist research reveals that at every period of church history there were women engaging in leadership roles. Even during the patristic period, when the Fathers of the Church were affirming the inferiority of women, there were ascetic women who opted out of the traditional woman's role. Rosemary Ruether notes that these women were "writers, thinkers, Scripture scholars, and innovators in the formation of monastic life." Unfortunately, because they were women their leadership ability was never acknowledged.

By the Middle Ages, however, some women had begun to assume leadership roles, sometimes exercising even greater influence than the local bishop. When we hear their stories, we can imagine that, at least in the imaginations of those who observed them, they challenged the idea that all women were inferior.

Most prominent among these were the Beguines and the abbesses. The Beguines lived a semi-monastic life in houses they established on the outskirts of towns, beginning in Belgium in the twelfth century. They quickly spread to Germany, England, and France, until by the end of the thirteenth century they were a feature in almost every town. The Great Beguinage at Ghent had thousands of inhabitants, two churches, eighteen convents, over 100 houses and a brewery and an infirmary. Undoubtedly, the women in the beguinages had influence on the townspeople.

The abbesses of the Middle Ages often exercised roles that were thought to belong exclusively to males. For example, Jeanne-Baptiste de Bourbon of the Abbey of Fontevrault nominated her own clergy and paid the benefices for their forty rectories, chapels and churches. The abbesses picked their own priors, giving them the authority to preach. They chanted the divine office and presided over all religious services, except the Mass. Abbesses in Germany and England also had seats and votes in their nations' parliaments.

There were women religious scholars in the Middle Ages, though it was not until the twentieth century that the church bestowed the title of Doctor of the Church on St. Catherine of Siena and St. Teresa of Avila. St. Catherine was a theologian, a reformer and a mystic; but, according to Eleanor McLaughlin, she exercised her influence through her holiness. The impression these women must have made on those who encountered them is obvious in a remark attributed to Teresa's bishop: ''That woman should have been a man.''

Following in the leadership footsteps of their medieval predecessors came the religious women of the Counter-Reformation period. The religious communities established by women like Louise de Marillac to help the poor, Mother Clarke to teach the immigrant children, and Mother Cabrini to care for the sick have made an invaluable contribution to the religious life of the Catholic community. In the process they have done much to dispel the myth that women cannot exercise leadership. They established schools, hospitals, orphanages and social service agencies. They raised money to support their communities and generally acted as heads of their various projects. They were role models for the children they taught, especially when they offered educational opportunities to young women who might otherwise have been denied an education.

The memory of these women remains today as a sign that at every time in the church's history there were women who, by their lives, challenged the narrowness of the ideas about sexuality in both the church and the culture. They were the embodiment in every period of the church of the special significance of the Blessed Mother in the Catholic tradition: if one woman does not fit the stereotype, then it can't be "natural" for women to be inferior.

Perhaps these women were inspired by the minor, though firmly entrenched, tendency of some writers, especially the mystics, to refer to the femininity of God. During the apostolic age and well into the Middle Ages, the idea of the femininity of God persisted in the orthodox writings of Augustine, Anselm and Mechtild as well as in the apocryphal and gnostic writings. Church art also supported the view of a feminine dimension of God. Julian of Norwich, the fifteenth century mystic, spoke of Jesus as Mother.

In addition, while the theologians and Church leaders often reflected a negative attitude on sexuality, there are hints that at the imagination level of religious experience the sacramentality of sexuality was recognized. The imaginations of the faithful who participated in these rituals were exposed to a positive view of sexuality despite the condemnations of sexual activity being pronounced by the theologians.

One example of this positive image of sexuality that has survived even in our modern liturgy is found in the ritual of the Easter Vigil. The plunging of the Easter Candle into the water while praying that the candle will fructify the water uses the symbol of intercourse to capture the relationship of Christ to the community of believers.

Another example is found in the various marriage blessings that developed as the clergy began to bless the marital unions of the faithful. A blessing for the veiling of the bride that dates to the fourth or fifth century acknowledges the sacramentality of the "work" of the marriage created by God. And the blessing for the veiling of the bride in the *Gregorian Sacramentary* of the seventh century refers to marriage as the society blessed in the beginning by God with a blessing that was never taken away either by original sin or the Flood.

In conclusion, the history of the church's attitudes on sexuality demonstrates how difficult it has been for church leaders and theologians to develop the idea of sexuality as more than sex. As our smorgasbord approach to that history makes clear, reactions to external pressures have often dictated the focus of church discussions on sexuality. Perhaps because of that, the theology and the laws of the church on sexuality did not move far beyond the narrow perspective of the patriarchal culture in which the church had its beginnings. The contemporary church needs to be mindful of the important values of sacramentality and marriage and family that are part of the Tradition on sexuality, but it also must recognize that each new age brings different questions to the faith, questions that can't always be answered with past formulae.

CHAPTER IV
The Magisterium Since Vatican II

. . . the morality of sexual acts between married people takes its meaning first of all and specifically from the ordering of their actions in a fruitful married life, that is, one which is practiced with responsible, generous, and prudent parenthood. It does not then depend upon the direct fecundity of each and every particular act.

> The Majority Report of the Papal
> Commission on Birth Control

. . . "each and every marital act must remain open to the transmission of life."

> *Humanae Vitae*

THERE is a story, now more a legend, about Pope John XXIII's decision to call the Second Vatican Council. He is reputed to have flung open a window in his quarters, claiming as he did so that the Vatican needed to open the windows of the church and let in some fresh air. Whether or not the pope actually said this, it is true that the Council was called to examine how the church might speak to the modern world in which it no longer exercised the influence it had enjoyed in previous eras.

Whether what has happened in the church since the Council is a direct result of the Council or whether it might have happened even if there had never been a council is open to debate. But it is a debate that can never reach a definitive conclusion. The Council did take place and did attempt changes in response to the understandings of the modern world. And there have been enormous changes in the church and in people's attitude toward the church since that time. Most discussions of Catholicism consider the Council a benchmark, using pre-Vatican II and post-Vatican II as indicators of different ideas and attitudes about the church and its role.

Our search for guidelines for a positive Catholic vision of sexuality turns to the statements of the magisterium during and after Vatican II. We examine them to see how they either help or hinder the bringing together of the experience of sexuality and the wisdom of the Catholic faith.

When we analyze these statements we want to know if the anti-sex, anti-woman attitude of the past has been discarded, if the church leaders realize that sexuality is more than sex, if the natural law basis of evaluations of sexual behavior has been expanded to include an understanding of "natural" as more than physical, if the experience of married people is taken into consideration when directives about marital intimacy are issued, if sexual sins are no longer *the* sins, if sacramental marriage is seen as a covenant relationship rather than a contract relationship, if the personhood of woman is acknowledged, if women's experiences are considered as sources of revelation, if reproduction is no longer the primary focus of marital intimacy, and if the focus of the teachings has moved away from concentration on sexual morality and toward proclamation of vision.

Unless our examination reveals a positive response to all these questions, the difference between pre- and post-

Vatican II church teachings will not make much difference in the magisterium's ability to create a vision that speaks to the experience of sexuality in the contemporary world.

In this brief review of some key magisterium teachings we will look at a statement on marital sexuality in documents of Vatican II, several important pronouncements since that time, directives in response to positions taken by the faithful on sexuality issues, and, finally, a theology of the body and sexuality developed by Pope John Paul II. This is not an exhaustive study of the contemporary teachings of the magisterium; however, we can discern much about the present attitude of the magisterium on sexuality from an examination of these sources.

Vatican II on Marital Sexuality

The Pastoral Constitution on the Church (*Gaudium et Spes*) acknowledged that conjugal love is the foundation of marriage and that the bond between men and women is the sacramental basis of the marriage. Conjugal love which is directed by the will from one person to another involves the good of the whole person; in this way it enriches the mind and body with a unique dignity. The constitution also maintained that by their very nature marriage and conjugal love are ordained for the procreation and education of children, who are the ultimate crown of the relationship.

However, parents are called to be "cooperators with the love of God" and "interpreters of that love." They are not simply to propagate, but they are to procreate. Responsible parenthood is required of all. The decision about what constitutes "responsible parenthood" is left to the parents themselves, who "make this judgment in the sight of God" and "in light of the total welfare of the persons involved." This document reflects the "collegial" approach of a conciliar statement.

PRONOUNCEMENTS

Humanae Vitae

The collegial approach of *Gaudium et Spes* did not extend to the church's teaching on artificial birth control. The Council did not treat the subject of artificial birth control, leaving it to consideration by the pope. The subject was also removed from the agenda of the Synod of Bishops of 1967. Instead, in 1968, Pope Paul VI, after consulting with the commission established to consider the teaching on birth control, issued the encyclical *Humanae Vitae,* a papal letter reiterating the church's stand against artificial contraception. The encyclical was a reaffirmation of the teaching authority of the pope and of the traditional natural law understanding of sexuality.

In issuing the letter, the pope went against the opinion of the majority of members of the Papal Commission on Birth Control, who held that the morality of sexual acts between married people was not dependent on the "direct fecundity of each and every particular act;" rather, this morality flows "first of all and specifically from the ordering of their actions in a fruitful married life," one in which they practiced "responsible, generous, and prudent parenthood." In their opinion, contraception should be evaluated in relation to the other human values operative in the marriage.

In rebuttal of this position Pope Paul insisted that the teaching of the magisterium prohibiting artificial contraception is founded on "the inseparable connection, willed by God" of the unitive and procreative meanings of the conjugal act. This connection cannot be broken "by man on his own initiative." For this reason, "each and every marriage act must remain open to the transmission of life." Rhythm may be permitted because it adheres to the natural laws of the generative process (the biological laws, the critics point out).

Although the unitive and procreative meanings of marriage are linked in this presentation, it only sees an interference with the physical act of procreation as destroying the meaning of marriage. The document does not reflect a consideration of the experience of marital intimacy which is both physical and psychological.

Declaration on Sexual Ethics

In December 1975, the Sacred Congregation for the Doctrine of the Faith issued its Declaration on Certain Questions Concerning Social Ethics. A positive feature of this document is its emphasis on the importance of marriage and family life and its belief that genital sexual activity finds its deepest meaning in the context of marriage. In addition, the declaration exhibits a pastoral sensitivity that has not always been present in church prohibitions against certain sexual practices.

However, when the statement addresses certain questions—pre-marital sex, masturbation, and homosexuality—sexuality again becomes physical sex. Even though the document does not claim to address all questions relative to sexuality and acknowledges that it is dealing with questions of sexual ethics, it does so after a very limited presentation of an incomplete vision of sexuality. Again, sexual ethics is the focus of a church statement.

Ordination of Women

The hope that the Catholic Church might eventually open its priesthood to women was dashed in January of 1977 when the Vatican released the Declaration on the Question of the Admission of Women to the Ministerial Priesthood, a "definitive" statement of the theological basis for the non-ordination of women. According to this statement, Christ intended to exclude women from ordination; and this exclusion is basic to the church's understanding of priesthood. The declaration claimed that the exclusion of women was not related to any idea of their inferiority, since the church has always believed in the equality of women (which, needless to say, was a surprise to most women). Due to the Tradition of the church, women could not be admitted to the priesthood. Citing the theological link between Christ, maleness, and priesthood, the declaration affirmed that it would be impossible to deviate from this tradition.

One reads this declaration and wonders if those who framed it were at all aware of the situation of women in the modern world or of the scientific insights into sexuality or of biblical research that would question their interpretation of Christ's intention. One also wonders how they fail to see that their position is a reinforcement of the stereotype of woman as inferior.

Familiaris Consortio

After the Synod of the Bishops on the Family of 1980, Pope John Paul II issued *Familiaris Consortio,* which included many of the conclusions of the Synod's participants along with some of his own reflections on the issues they discussed. Key statements in the document relate to the special charism of married couples, the changing role of women, the importance of the domestic church, and the reiteration of the church's teaching on birth control.

The pope emphasized that the charism of the sacrament of matrimony makes it possible for lay married people, using the wisdom that comes from their marriage, to make a unique and indispensable contribution to the church's theology of marriage. This assertion indicated that the experience of marriage, as articulated by married people, is a legitimate reference for theological reflection.

Some American bishops who were pastorally aware of the damage done by *Humanae Vitae* and of the rejection of the church's teachings on birth control had been listening to the charism of the married laity and felt that the issue of birth control should be re-examined. Having read the pre-Synod draft statement, they also were aware of the negative attitude of some Vatican officials on married sexuality. References to "unbridled passion" had drawn criticism from many who had read the draft statement. During the Synod, Archbishop Quinn of San Francisco made an intervention (probably on the part of the American bishops) which was a thinly disguised request for a re-examination of the teaching on birth control.

Familiaris Consortio clearly rejected the thought that such a re-examination would be possible. Pope John

Paul II reaffirms *Humanae Vitae.* Asserting that the only morally acceptable form of birth prevention is that which uses the natural cycle, he cites the claim of "numerous" married people that the planning necessary to use this method (practicing control in their conjugal relations) enriches them spiritually.

Critics of this papal analysis observe that while this might be true for the couples he referred to, it does not mean that it would be true for all married couples or that this control might not, at times, be detrimental to a marriage. Here, as in *Humanae Vitae,* the church displays a lack of appreciation of the role of sexual intimacy in a long-term marital relationship.

At the same time, there appears to be a fear that the ordinary lay person will fall prey to "unbridled passion" unless the church points out the dangers of artificial birth control. We agree that it is possible that some people will act irresponsibly when they do not have to fear pregnancy as a consequence of their activity. Still, this does not validate the church's refusal to investigate how sexual intimacy plays a healing and enriching role in a marriage.

On the subject of women's changing role in the world, prodded by a position paper worked out by a group of American observers, the Synod called attention to the need to recognize the new opportunities for women and also some of the obstacles society puts in the way of women's advancement. The pope included this idea in his statement, emphasizing that women should have the freedom to choose whether they wanted to remain in the home or become involved in the work force. In either case, they should not have to suffer hardship as a result of their choice. However, neither the bishops nor the pope extended this freedom to choose to roles within the church.

Disciplinary Actions

A series of directives from Rome addressing issues in the American Church in the 1980's as well as actions by some American bishops during this same period raise serious questions about whether the magisterium of this time has any desire to move beyond the law in its pronouncements on sexuality. In particular, the Vatican actions against women's religious orders, against a theologian who has raised questions about non-infallible teachings on sexuality, its stripping of a bishop's authority on sexual matters, its attempt to suppress the results of a survey of bishops regarding their opinions on sexuality issues, its pressure on bishops to work against anti-discrimination measures for homosexuals, and its 1986 letter to the world's bishops reaffirming its teaching on homosexuality along with the pope's repeated references to the evils of artificial contraception all reinforce the image of the church as negative about sexuality.

In addition, American bishops who have banned altar girls, who support political candidates who agree with them on sexuality issues even when they favor capital punishment and nuclear armament (two positions the bishops oppose), who oppose anti-discrimination measures for homosexuals, and who react to every complaint against writers or speakers by someone who charges them with laxity about sexual morality do not project a positive church stance on sexuality. Jesus was a vision-giver; the representatives of his church in the contemporary world are better known as lawmakers.

Theology of the Body and Sexuality

We might ask at this juncture whether it is possible for the church to be a vision-giver when it comes to the subject of sexuality. Is there any way out of this negative image church leaders have when it comes to sexuality? Where might they begin? One example of how the magisterium might be able to bring together the experience of sexuality and the light of faith is the theology of the body and sexuality developed by Pope John Paul II.

Despite the pope's resolute support of the Tradition on matters of sexual morality and on women in ministry, he has developed a theology of the body and sexuality that provides the strongest support ever to emanate from the official church for a positive vision of sexuality. Unfortunately, there often is an inconsistency between what the pope presents as his theology and the way in which he then uses this theology to support the Tradition's "natural law" understanding of morality and its exclusion of women from ordination.

Still, the theology is an appeal to the religious imagination in its phenomenological, personalist, and poetic reflections on sexuality in light of the Catholic faith. At the abstract, theological level, the pope engages in the correlating of experience and faith that is necessary if the church is to provide guidelines on sexuality.

Beginning in September of 1979 (one year before the Bishops' Synod on the Family) and continuing through April of 1981 (the week before the assassination attempt), the pope presented fifty-six audience addresses on a theology of sexuality and the body. After his recovery from the attack, he began the application of this theology to a discussion of marriage, celibacy and virginity. Then, in the summer and fall of 1984, he concluded his reflections on sexuality by applying his theology to a consideration of sexual ethics, especially birth control.

For our purpose, we will examine the theology developed in the first fifty-six addresses, since it contains the most original and visionary ideas on sexuality to ever come out of the Vatican. The way the pope rushes to apply this theology to sexual ethics without listening to his own advice about the charism of married people simply reinforces our contention that the magisterium's concern with sexual morality sorely limits its ability to deal with the problems of sexuality in the contemporary world.

One could argue, as I do elsewhere, that there are other pastoral applications of the pope's theology than the one he chooses. Using his theology as a basis for a spirituality of sexuality would make for a much more positive statement on sexuality than the ones the pope makes when he applies it to sexual morality.

Following Jesus' directive to the Pharisees to look to the "beginning" to discover why divorce is forbidden, the pope analyzes the first four chapters of Genesis. He incorporates recent scientific and psychological understandings of human sexuality and arrives at the conclusion that, from our religious perspective, sexuality is "the basic fact of human existence."

The story told by the Genesis authors—and alluded to by Jesus—deals with God's plan that sexuality be the vehicle for the continuation of divine revelation. Alone in the

Garden, neither Adam nor Eve could have discovered his or her true identity, could have known the meaning of life, could have been "in the image of God." Together, in a state of grace, they were able to know God's plan. When they "clung together" and became "two in one flesh," they became aware of their power to be "in the image of God."

In the pope's opinion, this story attests to the goodness of sexuality and the body, and of sexuality's ability to help people join their differences (masculinity and femininity) in a way that together they mirror the God who created them in his image, male *and* female. This joining together is an affirmation of the personhood of woman, since it is only in a communion of persons that humans can reflect God's love. Women's experiences are as valid as men's for revealing the God in whose image they are both created. In fact, God is known more fully when the two experiences are resources for speaking of God.

Along with the gift (grace) of the body and sexuality, God gave man and woman the freedom to choose whether or not to live according to the divine plan. When they chose to reject God's plan, they gave up the "innocence" that allowed them to be a "communion of persons;" but they did not lose their desire to be that "image of God." The story of life after the fall is the story of the ongoing struggle to live in a relationship of persons (each a subject) as opposed to a "relationship of appropriation" (one or both as objects).

But Jesus came to bring the "redemption of the body," to remind humankind of how life was when people lived in a graced relationship with God and to offer them the grace to live life according to God's plan. Jesus' interpretation of God's plan for sexuality became apparent to the pope when he reflected on the prohibition against adultery in the heart.

Contrary to the interpretation of "looking lustfully" and "adultery in the heart" as condemnations of impure thoughts, the pope interpreted Christ's words in the Sermon on the Mount as a call to rediscover the meaning of the body and sexuality in the "beginning." Adultery in the heart means existing in a relationship of appropriation where one or both partners are objects. No communion of persons can exist unless both partners are persons, are subjects. Anyone who uses another person only as a sex object is as guilty of adultery as someone who actually has intercourse with someone to whom he or she is not married. And using someone as a "sex object" goes beyond just physical sexual relations.

According to the pope's analysis, the grace of the Spirit that Jesus left to his followers is the grace that will help them be aware of God's plan; also, this grace will assist them when they try to live according to the plan. Even when they fail, as all will do from time to time, the grace of their bodies is a reminder to them that there is a deeper meaning to life.

Although the audience addresses, written in a scholarly language, are difficult to understand, they can be used as a resource for those who might want to develop a vision that brings together experience and faith. They contain a wealth of ideas that would be useful for homilies, marriage education, sex education, and the development of a spirituality of sexuality.

Within these teachings of the magisterium, we find contradictions between the theoretical and positive statements on human sexuality and the negative tone of many prohibitions related to sexual activity. This reflects the confusion that results when a heavy emphasis is placed on sexual morality.

In this era of mass communication and increased levels of education, church statements are subjected to a much wider critique than they were in previous ages.

When a document is written in a formal tone using philosophical and theological language, many of its nuances are lost on audiences that are not familiar with this language. Arguments are summarized in short statements that can be understood by readers of the popular press. And from that point on, the short statements, not always reflective of the essence of the document, come to represent the core of the document. At this time, no matter what positive things a church statement might have to say about sexuality, if it also contains prohibitions that do not seem to have any relationship to the experience of sexuality, only the prohibitions will be noted. And, once again, the church will be dismissed as a viable participant in discussions of human sexuality.

The magisterium will communicate the Good News about sexuality effectively only when it begins to realize that its emphasis on sexual morality is not only ineffective; it also is not vision-giving, as the Good News should be.

CHAPTER V
Sexuality in the 1980's

. . . to assert that pleasure for women—sexual pleasure unburdened by meaning—is a legitimate social goal.

> Thesis attributed to authors of *Remaking Love* by reviewer, Judith Viorst
> October, 1986

It is only in the marital relationship that the use of the sexual faculty can be morally good. A person engaging in homosexual behavior therefore acts immorally.

> Letter from the Congregation for the Doctrine of the Faith to all bishops
> October, 1986

Pre-marital sex is wrong—agree Young adults 12%
                                Ages 35-54 . . . . 48%
                                55 & older 76%

> Results of an opinion survey in a Chicago parish
> November, 1986

AT this point in our search for guidelines for sexuality, we have to ask if knowing the magisterium's present pronouncements on the subject is sufficient help for our task. Today, when people have access to considerable information about sexuality, have the freedom to make their own choices about how to live as sexual persons, and know the church's rules about correct sexual behavior, are they sufficiently prepared for dealing with any sexuality-related questions they might face?

If the voice of the magisterium were the only voice—or even the only Catholic voice—addressing the topic of sexuality, we could have concluded our discussion of guidelines with the previous chapter. The church has spoken. If the faithful would accept these teachings as the word of God, they would come to know the true meaning of sexuality. However, now, as in the past, there is a level of discussion about sexuality other than that of the official church. We would not have a complete background for determining a Catholic understanding of sexuality without considering this contemporary thinking in some detail.

There is both a secular and a religious debate about sexuality. An examination of both these debates supports our earlier claim that there is no simple answer to the complexity of human sexuality. The contemporary discussion, both in secular society and in the church, makes it clear that sexuality still is a mystery force in human life and undoubtedly will remain so for the foreseeable future.

Both the secular debate and the discussions within the Catholic community have a theoretical component and what we could call a practical component. At the theoretical level, opinions are offered by a wide variety of thinkers ranging from academics who have done research on the topic to magazine writers who popularize the latest research to talk show hosts who express their conclusions about the meaning of sexuality, oftentimes not aware that they are doing that. In short, there is no lack of discussion about sexuality-related issues.

At the practical level, people live out their sexual lives often unaware that their behavior indicates their understanding of the meaning of sexuality. Still, when we consider how people (including Catholics) live their sexual lives, we can discern some contemporary attitudes about sexuality.

The Secular Debate

Two positions predominate within the secular debate. The "sex without meaning" position proposed by the authors of *Re-making Love* sums up a variety of views that seek to separate human sexuality from anything other than individual sexual actions. The American Medical Association's position that sexuality is "more" than sex is representative of the other stance.

The first position is related to the support of sex without responsibility and sex without commitment. In both cases, sexual activity is seen as separate from any other human need. Though its proponents might claim they support sex without meaning, they are in fact assigning a meaning to sexual activity—sex means instant gratification for the individual and nothing more than that.

Though this view of the meaning of sexuality was implicit in the "double standard" that allowed men to be sexually active both prior to marriage and with other than a spouse during marriage, it became more widely acceptable once women were able to have sex without pregnancy. And now that women no longer need the protection offered by

the genetic inclination to bonding with the father of an offspring, they are being encouraged to "enjoy" sex with "no
strings attached." For some this means to approach sex
like a man supposedly does, free from responsibility.

From this perspective sex is unrelated to bonding or to
reproduction, and it has no implications for male and
female roles. The psychological emphasis is on self-fulfill-
ment. The sexual drive is acknowledged as a powerful instinct, but is seen as a drive that is best satisfied when
unencumbered. The logical implication of this thinking is
that the modern woman should be a playgirl, just as the
man is a playboy. The previous objectification of a person
—the woman in the "girlie" magazines—is now extended
to men. Manifestations of this notion of sexuality abound
in some "acceptable" contemporary behavior and in many
destructive sexual relationships.

Sexual activity among the young is one example of how
society's emphasis on instant sexual gratification has had
devastating results. The glamour of the media portrayal of
sex without meaning quickly fades when a young girl is
faced with the effects of sex without responsibility. The
media personalities who live together without the benefit
of marriage and who give birth to babies out of wedlock
don't face the bleak future that awaits many sexually active teenagers.

According to a report from the United States Depart-
ment of Health and Human Services, there were nearly
10,000 births to girls under 15 in 1982. And in the same
year, out of every 10,000 white, unmarried 15-17 year olds,
there were nearly 3,200 who were sexually active, 600 who
became pregnant, 200 who gave birth, and 120 who raised

their babies as single mothers. Among black girls the numbers were even higher: 5,400 out of every 10,000 were sexually active, 1,400 became pregnant, 700 gave birth, and 600 opted to raise their children without a father. And these statistics don't even begin to reveal the impact of early sexual activity on a young person's ability to develop his/her sexual identity and capacity for intimacy.

Sexual abuse of children, rape, prostitution, pornography, sexual harassment in the workplace, job discrimination against women, and advertising that uses sexual manipulation as its sole basis all can be traced to an understanding of sexuality that objectifies a person. There is little in the way of romantic love—love that sees the other as a person to be respected—in many of our society's messages about sexuality. Both theoretically and practically the idea of sex without meaning has a strong hold on the imagination of our society.

A more wholistic understanding of sexuality is proposed by those who support the second secular position. The psychological implications of masculinity and femininity are taken into consideration. There is a call for sexual maturity and for an integrated sexual identity. Women are considered to be partners in a relationship rather than objects who behave in stereotypic ways. People are urged to assume responsibility for their sexual behavior and for their sexual identity. Freedom of choice is applauded; but its corollary, responsibility for the results of one's choices, is also emphasized.

In some instances, proponents of this perspective acknowledge the psychological drive toward intimacy and view sexual behavior as enriching the capacity for intimacy. One's partner in sexual activities is seen as an individual whose needs should be taken into consideration. Pregnancy as a result of sexual activity should be a mutually arrived at decision (though for many the discontinuation of a pregnancy is a decision that rests with the woman alone).

At a practical level this view of sexuality is seen in much of what could be called the "sexuality sells" approach to publishing and advertising. Standing in the checkout lines at the supermarket, one can see how the advertisers and publishers recognize the human desire to be successful in every area of life affected by sexuality. The covers of magazines promise the reader that s/he will learn to be a successful physical and psychological partner, to be sexually attractive, to be a role model and a sex educator for the young, to be a successful working woman and a tender, involved father. Sexuality is seen as "more than sex."

However, putting a wholistic understanding of sexuality into practice is an ongoing challenge even for those who accept it in theory. There are some people who respect the personhood of their sexual partner, others who try to set an example of responsible sexual behavior for the young, some who resist pressure to manipulate anyone sexually, and still others who strive for meaningful sexual relationships in which they combine commitment and playfulness; but to do all these things all of the time is difficult. And though, for many people, the desire to have an integrated sexual identity is strong, the reality of life as a sexual being often makes this seem an arduous task.

The secular debate actually points out the fallacy of believing that scientific understanding of sexuality will provide the ultimate answer to how to live as a sexually mature human being. Armed with research on the physical and psychological dimensions of sexuality, participants in this debate come up with divergent conclusions. Sexuality, though not mysterious for the modern in the same way as it was for previous generations, continues to mystify. There still is a need to know how sexuality relates to what one considers the "ultimate" meaning of human existence. Theoretically, religious discussions of the meaning of sexuality attempt to do this relating.

The Catholic Debate

The controversy surrounding sexuality in Catholic circles not directly related to the magisterium also has a practical and theoretical side. Practically, there are Catholics who feel the final word on sexuality-related matters rests in the statements of the magisterium; and there are Catholics who have rejected the teachings of the magisterium on sexuality. Theoretically, there are those who, even when not agreeing with the magisterium, limit their discussions of sexuality to consideration of morally acceptable behavior; and there are those, few in number, who discuss a Catholic understanding of sexuality as sacramental and urge the development of a spirituality of sexuality. Before explaining this final position, which I believe is the correct basis for guidelines for sexuality, we will consider the other practical and theoretical views being debated among Catholics in the 1980's.

The Practical Level

Generally those who support the magisterium's positions on sexual morality as the *only* Catholic understand-

ing of sexuality believe that those who disagree with them
are not true Catholics. Organized supporters of this position have accepted an understanding of sexuality based on
the rules of the church and have appointed themselves the
guardians of the rules, attacking anyone who does not
agree with their interpretation of the rules. They do not, in
most instances, have an integrated understanding of sexuality. Rather, they see sexuality issues as being sex,
reproduction, and the non-ordination of women; and they
accept the magisterium's teaching on these issues as the
revealed word of God.

Those who accept the rules approach as the best Catholic response to the mystery of sexuality have invested their
understanding of faith in the claim that the church has
always taught those principles of sexual morality which are
based on the teachings of Jesus. Any suggestion that there
is more to sexuality than sex and sexual morality is seen as
a threat to the teaching authority of the church and in
many instances as a threat to the individual's understanding of faith. When sexual behavior becomes the chief criterion of faith, the believer is bound to encounter difficulties with his/her own ability to adhere to rules and with
the larger society that does not accept the rules.

An extreme example of this position was the middle-
aged woman who confronted me privately prior to a lecture for a group of young adults on sexuality. She questioned me as to whether I accepted the pope's teaching on
birth control. When I asked what her question had to do
with my lecture, she informed me that she had seven young
adult children and two of them had been "ruined" by
priests who had not agreed with the pope on birth control.
Her only concern was with my acceptance of this teaching.

At almost every lecture I give on sexuality a "guardian of the faith" is present, evaluating whether what I say is acceptable church teaching. Since I do not address sexual morality in my lectures, they seldom find fault with what I say, even when it is a serious challenge to their "morality only" understanding of sexuality.

The problem with this approach to sexuality is not with its acceptance of the magisterium's teaching, but with its failure to realize that sexual morality teachings alone will never help people live their sexuality in a positive manner. If the experience of the past teaches us nothing else, it at least proves that following rules does not lead to growth in appreciation of the positive possibilities of sexuality. The rules approach to sexuality allowed an anti-sex, anti-woman mentality to dominate the church's thinking for most of its history. With that attitude, the sacramentality of sexuality was never allowed to surface. If the church is ever going to make a positive contribution to discussions about human sexuality, something more than rules for correct sexual behavior is needed.

That something more is needed is also obvious when we consider the large percentage of Catholics who disagree with the magisterium's teachings on sexual morality. Increasingly, these Catholics are not opting out of participation in church activities; but they no longer listen to the magisterium on sexuality-related issues. These people do not necessarily have any better appreciation of the need for an integrated understanding of sexuality than do those who accept the teachings of the magisterium. They simply find the arguments supporting the magisterium's pronouncements to be contrary to their experience of sexuality. And since they associate the church leadership's approach to sexuality with negative pronouncements, they have little interest in what the church has to say about sexuality.

The majority of American Catholics reject the church's prohibition against artificial contraception. In 1984 nine out of ten Catholics and four out of five weekly communicants did not agree with the statement that artificial birth control is wrong, and this despite the repeated statements of the pope about the evils of contraception.

The significance of these statistics is even more apparent when we consider the results of a survey of opinions in one Chicago parish. In many respects this parish would be considered "conservative" or "traditional" in its approach to religion. Only 21% of the respondents in a randomly selected group thought women should be ordained, 56% thought priests/nuns should ALWAYS wear distinctive garb, and 31% believed that EVERYTHING in the Bible is literally true.

However when it came to questions on their sexual values, their support of church teachings dropped considerably. Only 16% of the respondents thought divorce and remarriage and artificial birth control were wrong. The percentages jumped to 55% against pre-marital sex and 56% against abortion and jumped even higher on adultery, with 88% disapproving. As our opening quote indicates, there is a significant difference in the attitudes of the young, the middle-aged, and the elderly on pre-marital sex, with only 12% of young adults agreeing it was wrong. If acceptance of the magisterium's sexual morality were to be the criterion for membership, this parish would have very few members.

Neither the supporters of the magisterium's teachings nor those who reject them can be faulted for their failure to see that the Catholic heritage might have something positive to say about the mystery encountered in life as a sexual being in the contemporary world. The clergy have not made a concerted effort to use the wisdom of the heritage as a way of challenging people. Aware of the faithful's rejection of the teaching on sexual morality, many clergy fear that any discussion of sexuality will end up with questions on their opinions on these teachings, opinions that are fairly close to those of the faithful. Unwilling to go on public record against the teachings, the clergy refrain from any discussion of sexuality. As a result the "discussion" of sexuality at the practical level revolves around the magisterium's teachings on sexual behavior.

Another practical debate about the meaning of sexuality is apparent in the response of many Catholics to the church's anti-woman mentality, apparent in the prohibitions against women in liturgical functions. When pastors and bishops carry this prohibition to the extreme of forbidding altar girls, mothers and fathers, more conscious of sex discrimination than they were in the past, become irate. To them this is just one more manifestation that the church is out of touch with the world on matters of sexuality. These people find themselves becoming more and more open to the critiques of the magisterium presented by feminist thinkers.

In summary, at the practical level, attitudes about sexuality among the Catholic faithful vary widely. But, generally speaking, there is little talk about a Catholic "imagination" on sexuality, or about sexuality as more than sex,

or about sexuality as sacramental and revelatory of God.
The faithful within the church and the outsider observing
the church still associate the church's wisdom about sexuality with its pronouncements on sexual morality.

THE THEORETICAL LEVEL

Sexual Morality

For the most part the scholarly discussions about sexuality in Catholic circles revolve around the same issues
that concern the magisterium. Even when many of those
engaged in these conversations are in disagreement with
the conclusions of church authorities, they still tend to
make sexual morality the focus of the debate.

Scholars go to great lengths to either prove or disprove
the scriptural, traditional, and natural law basis of the
magisterium's teachings on birth control, divorce, homosexuality, abortion, sterilization, celibacy, masturbation,
non-ordination of women, and, to a lesser degree, issues
related to biomedicine.

Books with titles that suggest a treatment of a Catholic
perspective on sexuality invariably address these issues,
continuing to equate sexuality with sex. Even when they
disagree with the magisterium's claim to be scripturally
based and true to the natural law in its pronouncements on
sexuality, they quickly move from a short presentation of a
more broadly based personalistic interpretation of human
nature to an evaluation of the specific behaviors outlawed
by the magisterium. Even when these books call for re-
evaluating the role of women in order to understand sex-

uality, they fail to carry through on the implication of this challenge.

For the most part, sexuality is still "sex" in these discussions. Here, too, there is little appeal to the imagination, either to the imagination to be uncovered in the rich Catholic heritage of sacramentality or to the imagination of the experience of sexuality. The sacramentality of sexuality and the opportunities for discovering and revealing God that are present in human sexuality are seldom considered. Even if the burden of the rules is removed, there is still little joy in this approach to a Catholic position on sexuality.

A crucial issue that is seldom given sufficient attention either by the magisterium or by those who write books on sexual morality is the situation of women. Scholarly discussion of the church's attitude toward women, however, is important for discovering how the church might respond to the challenge of sexuality in our contemporary world. Most of this discussion rejects the magisterium's teaching on women in ministry as well as many of the church's pronouncements on sexual morality.

The examination of woman's place in scripture and tradition and of the present anti-woman mentality of the magisterium is of critical importance. Until the church rids itself of its anti-woman attitude, it will have a difficult time appreciating how sexuality can be a God-revealing experience. The partnership of women and men that is necessary to make sexuality God-revealing will be possible only when women are seen as persons equal in worth to men and when their experiences are taken into account when looking for God's revelation in human experience.

Spirituality of Sexuality

A spirituality of sexuality evolves out of the meeting of the experience of sexuality and the sacramental tradition of the Catholic heritage. This spirituality does not reject the need for moral guidelines; but it also does not limit the Catholic contribution to an enriched appreciation of sexuality to laws about sexual behavior. It takes Jesus seriously when he said he came to fulfill the law, to help us discover the direction in which the law wishes us to move, to redeem us from our false understanding of the meaning of sexuality, and to give us the grace of the Spirit to live our sexuality in such a way that it is a revelation of divine love.

Pope John Paul II's theology of sexuality and the body demands this Catholic approach to sexuality. Even though for him a consideration of sexual behavior, especially condemnation of artificial birth control, is the logical conclusion of his theology, it is possible to find a more fruitful use of his theology in a spirituality of sexuality.

A few members of the hierarchy are on record as supporting this approach to sexuality. For example, in the 1970's when he was archbishop of Cincinnati, Joseph Cardinal Bernardin wrote about the need for a spirituality of sexuality; and at the Synod on the Family in 1980 he made an intervention calling for 1) "a richer, more positive theology of sexuality" and 2) "a spirituality of marital intimacy." Still, at the scholarly level and in the pronouncements of the magisterium, there is little attention given to this unique Catholic approach to the mystery of human sexuality.

A spirituality of sexuality, building on the vision that emerges when the experience of sexuality encounters the beliefs of the faith tradition, would help the church move away from its anti-woman and anti-sex attitudes. A consideration of the experience of sexuality forces the acknowledgment that sexuality is more than sex and that woman as person is a critical concept for the development of intimacy. The Catholic heritage of sacramentality responds to the positive possibilities of sexuality, properly understood, with the challenge to acknowledge that sexuality is sacramental and woman is an analog of God (God is like a mother, a wife, a daughter, a sister). Indeed, these two concepts—sexuality as sacramental and woman as analog of God—are critical features of the Genesis vision of sexuality, of Jesus' re-affirmation of that vision, and of a spirituality of sexuality.

In addition, a spirituality of sexuality would encourage Catholics to realize that there is a relationship between the way they live as sexual beings and what they believe about their God. The creed they profess on Sundays is a statement of belief in creation, incarnation, redemption, and grace; all these doctrines challenge the Catholic to acknowledge the sacramentality of sexuality and to lead a life that reflects this sacramentality. Any position that denies this sacramentality and rejects the personhood of woman is heretical. Positions that ignore this Catholic wisdom about sexuality fail to respond to the fullness of life Jesus demands of those who would follow him.

In summary, the contemporary secular and religious debate about sexuality is strongly influenced by previous attention to sexuality as sex, sexuality as moral behavior.

In some instances contemporary discussions are a reaction against the negativity that surrounded much of the previous attitude about sexuality. In other situations, it appears that the complexity of sexuality causes people to search for easy answers to sexuality concerns. Whatever the reasons, at both the theoretical and practical levels there is a reluctance to explore the "more" of sexuality.

The Catholic heritage of sacramentality challenges people to consider the way sexuality affects many areas of human experience. An emphasis on a spirituality of sexuality instead of a rules of sexual behavior stance would give contemporary Catholics and others living in the contemporary world meaningful guidelines for living as sexual beings.

CHAPTER VI
Religion and Sexuality in the 21st Century

Sexuality is the last great outpost of the extraordinary in human experience.

David Tracy

In the Sermon on the Mount Christ does not invite man to return to the state of original innocence . . . but he calls him to rediscover—on the foundation of the perennial and, so to speak, indestructible meanings of what is "human"—the living forms of the "new man."

Pope John Paul II, December 3, 1980

IF one were to attempt to name the continuous threads that run through the centuries of discussions about sexuality on the part of theologians and leaders of the Catholic Church, one would have to include at least the following points:

1) Attention has concentrated on sexuality as erotic behavior and as a means for reproduction.
2) The focus has been on what constitutes morally correct behavior.
3) The natural law has been a guiding principle.
4) Much of the discussion has been a reaction to the perceived moral crises of the times; little attention has been given to developing a vision of sexuality.

5) There was little in-depth analysis of the experience of sexuality.

6) The discussions mirror a distrust of physical sexuality.

7) A negative attitude toward women made it next to impossible to develop a theology based on the vision of Genesis 2.

8) Biblical resources were used out of context and even re-worked to prove the validity of certain stands.

9) The implications for sexuality of the doctrines of creation, incarnation, redemption, grace and the Holy Spirit were seldom considered.

10) A key tenet of Catholicism—the sacramentality of all creation, including sexuality—was not seen as a challenge to develop a positive view of sexuality.

The effects of this orientation on the official church of the twentieth century have made it impossible for the church to be a challenging voice in the midst of the modern confusion about sexuality. When its own members question the directives on sexuality issued by the Vatican and supported by many bishops, there are serious questions about the church's ability to proclaim the meaning of sexuality to anyone.

How then, we might ask, will it ever be possible to bring sexuality and faith together in order to uncover the religious dimension of sexuality? Will the church ever change its focus from that of total concentration on sexual ethics to that of a search for a vision of sexuality? Or when someone writes guidelines on sexuality for Catholics of the twenty-first century, will the magisterium still be focusing on rules for erotic behavior and reproduction?

Not being blessed with a crystal ball, I find it difficult to predict what will happen with the official church. However, several possible scenarios come to mind:

First of all, it is not impossible to imagine that the anti-sex, anti-woman attitude of many present-day church leaders will continue. The Vatican bureaucracy is a self-perpetuating institution and might easily pick new members with the same orientation. If this be the case, we may safely predict that the church will lose what little credibility it still has on sexuality. This will be especially true for the church in Third World countries that will be emerging into greater affluence. With higher levels of education, people in these countries will no longer assume the "uneducated lay person subservient to the all-knowing clergy" role. In addition, the church will be less and less open to discovering the possibility of a vision for sexuality.

A second imaginable development would be the election of a pope who will decide to change the rules on some of the key sexuality-related issues but who still will not see the need to develop a vision of sexuality out of the meeting of life and faith. Though this might cause initial positive comments in the media and from people outside the church, it will do little to assist those who are searching for the meaning of sexuality. If changes are not offered in the context of a vision, people will still be confused about their sexuality. Freedom from restraints in the secular society has not eased general anxiety about sexuality. There is little reason to expect that a removal of religious restraints would have any more positive effect.

A third but not very likely event would be a decision by church leaders to insist on adherence to the church's pronouncements on sexuality by all the faithful as a test for continuing membership. Although to many outsiders this seems to be the present stand of the Vatican, in reality there is little that can be done to enforce such a move without causing a schism. And much as some members of the Vatican bureaucracy and some conservative groups might want this course of action, it probably will not happen.

A fourth possibility is that a new pope might decide to refrain from issuing pronouncements on sexual morality for a period of time, during which he would encourage the development of a vision of sexuality that tried to correlate life and faith. Then, in light of the newly developed vision, he would encourage ongoing attempts to discern correct moral behavior. If this fourth scenario were to occur, there would be a climate within the church that would encourage a meeting of "eros" and "ethos" in the human heart. The church would then be in a position to make a positive contribution to the never-ending quest for the meaning of human sexuality. This scenario would be the best way to end the stagnation that presently exists in the official church deliberations on sexuality.

SEXUALITY AND THE DOMESTIC CHURCH

If I were a crystal ball gazer, I would predict that church leaders probably will follow the first approach. However, as we have observed before, there are two levels of religious development, that from above and that from below. The Spirit moves and reveals God's continuing presence both in the deliberations of the official church and in the experiences of the believing faithful. I predict that, if there is to be any change in the church's ability to offer wisdom about the meaning of sexuality, this wisdom will begin to take root in the local religious communities.

Local religious communities are the gathering places of members of the domestic churches—the church of the family. In *Familiaris Consortio* Pope John Paul II acknowledges the theological validity of these churches both for the family members and for the wider church that can learn much from the wisdom these members have to offer about human relationships, about intimacy, about love.

The domestic churches are the locale for their members' initial encounters with God and for their first realizations of their sexuality. As such they are the ideal location for fostering an appreciation of the sacramental potential of sexuality. While a youngster is absorbing his/her image of God from the attitudes of parents, s/he is also developing attitudes that will affect how s/he integrates his/her sexuality.

In the family a child develops a positive or negative bodily self-image, learns how to give and receive affection, discovers what a man is and what a woman is, acquires an image of appropriate family roles, receives a "sex education" (and quite possibly also is educated about physical sexuality), and begins to develop a sense of the place of the erotic in human relationships. And in the family an adult who has developed negative feelings about his/her sexuality can be enticed into more positive sentiments by a loving spouse and by the experience of parenthood.

The family builds the foundation upon which children build their personal "imagination" about sexuality. If the family experience respects the personhood of women, more than likely, when the child is confronted with either theory or behavior that asserts this personhood, he/she is not threatened.

The family experience of sexuality is also an experience of a search for meaning, a search that looks beyond the answers that can be supplied by the family. Also, husbands and wives who, according to *Familiaris Consortio,* have special insights to contribute to the church's quest to understand sexuality, gain these insights in the family environment. Obviously, the family is also the ideal locale for developing a spirituality of sexuality. But the family needs external supports to accomplish this.

When family members gather in local community, they bring with them the mystery they encounter in their lives as sexual beings. Sometimes they are conscious of their confusion; at other times, while not aware of their inability to lead integrated sexual lives, they are suffering from this inability. In this setting, the experience of sexuality is open to an encounter with faith. This encounter has two foci: the validity of the experience as it is lived by individuals is challenged by the faith; at the same time, the faith is tested for its insights into the meaning of the mystery of human sexuality.

If this challenge is recognized and responded to, then it will be possible to discern the presence of the Spirit in the experience of sexuality. A vision of sexuality, rooted in a faith perspective, will develop and be subject to continuing critique. And, since the local parish church is also linked to other local churches that together form the diocese that in turn is joined with other dioceses in the universal church, the Spirit encountered in the local meeting of sexuality and faith would move beyond the individual local parishes. Revelation from below would be linked with revelation from above. This dual-sided revelation is able to operate as a challenge to live one's sexuality in a positive way only when it sparks a spirituality of sexuality.

Pastoral Leader as Dual Prosecutor

The local pastoral leadership will be key if this method of responding to the quest for the meaning of sexuality is to be successful. People in pastoral leadership roles will serve in a linking capacity, bringing experience in touch with faith and shedding the light of faith on the darkness generated by confusion over the experience. The pastoral leader will need to be in touch both with the people of the community and with the richness of the religious tradition.

Sexuality is a mystery experience; it forces people to search for something more. Since any experience of mystery carries the possibility of an encounter with God, a mystery also becomes a possible symbol for revelation of the divine. The pastoral leader will need to be aware of how sexuality, like other polymorphous symbols, is more than what appears on the surface. Sexuality *is* more than sex, and the pastoral leader must appreciate this "more" in order to help community members search the depth of their experience of sexuality and uncover its rich meaning.

The local church must be conscious of how sexuality manifests its presence in a broad range of human experiences. The seven areas of life identified by the Committee on Human Sexual Development could serve as a starting point for parish reflections on sexuality.

The pastoral theologian who engages in systematic reflection on the meeting of life and faith will be a crucial resource for those in local pastoral leadership roles. At the same time, pastoral theologians must be attuned to the questions that pastoral leaders bring to them. In this way the local church leader plays a dual prosecutor role, asking both the faith tradition and the people of the community to be attuned to the depth of meaning below the surface of individual experiences of life as a sexual being.

Armed with the results of theological reflection on the experiences of sexuality, the local church leader can help the community identify a valid response to the issues that manifest themselves. In addition, the pastoral leader can initiate ways of celebrating the sacramental possibilities of sexuality, emphasizing the positive vision of Genesis 2 and encouraging a spirituality of sexuality.

There is a powerful grace offered through the experience of human sexuality. When that grace is ignored, the demon of misuse of sexuality is allowed to flourish. Still, the Spirit remains ready to be tapped. At the present time and for the foreseeable future, it appears that the best way of releasing the Spirit rests in a "theology/religion/revelation from below" vision of sexuality that nurtures a spirituality of sexuality.

CONCLUSION

In conclusion, at every time and in every place, human-kind has been confronted with the challenge of how to live as sexual beings. This challenge is no less forceful in an age of increased knowledge about sexuality or increased freedom from civil restraints on sexual activity. In many ways the problems are more obvious to those who would reflect on the situation. The Catholic religious heritage, with its emphasis on the sacramentality of all creation, has insights to contribute to this ongoing search for the meaning of sexuality. Although an overemphasis on sexual morality as the only focus for religious input has damaged the church's ability to be a credible voice on sexuality issues, the wisdom of the vision inherent in the Catholic tradition would be a refreshing contribution to the present debate.

Contemporary Catholics, familiar with both the background of the church's attitudes on sex and women and with the vision of sexuality developed in Genesis and reiterated by Jesus, ought to be better able to demand a new focus to church discussions of sexuality. If they are to respond to what Pope John Paul II called Christ's invitation to rediscover the "living forms of the 'new man,'" they must be allowed to participate in meaningful reflections on the experience of sexuality, aided by the light that faith offers to their search.

It is time for the church to be about the Father's (and the Mother's) business of proclaiming the Good News about the divine plan for human sexuality. Then perhaps a twenty-first century magazine editor will be anxious to accept an article on how religion helps people lead sexually fulfilling lives.

DISCUSSION QUESTIONS

1) How do most people respond to discussions of sexuality? What reasons might they have for their reactions?

2) What is the opinion of persons both inside and outside the Catholic Church on the church's attitude on sexuality? How have they formed this opinion, and how valid is it?

3) Why do people experience confusion over sexuality?

4) How would you characterize our society's views on sexuality? What are some representative examples of these views?

5) Why would David Tracy say that sexuality is the last great outpost of the extraordinary in human experience?

6) What does "sexuality is more than sex" mean to you? How important is it to consider the implications of this idea?

7) Why is it necessary to examine the experience of sexuality if we want to develop a religious perspective on it? Why isn't it enough to repeat what has been taught in previous eras?

8) How does the Bible serve as a "prosecutor" of the meaning we asign to sexuality? How does our experience of ourselves as sexual beings "prosecute" the Bible? What might result from this mutual prosecution?

9) Why is it important to know the context of the biblical and traditional teachings on sexuality? What are some different perspectives on these teachings that can be gained from this approach?

10) What influence have the negative attitudes towards sex and women found in the Bible had on past and recent teachings on sexuality? How much attention has been given to the more positive views in the Bible? Which view has predominated?

11) Why did the Catholic Church, almost from its very beginnings, opt to emphasize a negative view of sexuality? How important are the positive views that have managed to exist alongside the negative ones?

12) What indications are there that this anti-sex, anti-woman attitude continues in our contemporary secular world? What are the roots of this attitude? What connection is there between an anti-woman and an anti-sex posture?

13) How does the Catholic Church demonstrate an anti-woman attitude? In what way does this influence the church's teachings on sexual morality?

14) What changes might occur in the Catholic Church's views on sexuality if church leaders adopted the view that "sexuality is more than sex"?

15) How might an understanding of the genetic basis of human sexuality influence the church's sexual morality teachings?

16) How does sexuality affect the seven areas of human experience enumerated by the Committee on Human Sexual Development? What are some positive effects of our understanding of sexuality in each of these areas? What are some negative effects?

17) How could Pope John Paul II's theology of sexuality and the body be applied to the experience of sexuality in our world today? What might it say about the seven areas of human experience?

18) What influence will the Catholic Church have in the future if leaders and theologians continue to concentrate on "sex" and reproduction in their statements on sexuality?